AMSTERDAM *MADE EASY* ✺

Andy Herbach

Author of *Paris Made Easy, Provence Made Easy,*
and co-author of the
Eating & Drinking on the Open Road guides

Open Road Publishing

Open Road Publishing

We offer travel guides to American and foreign locales. Our books tell it like it is, often with an opinionated edge, and our experienced authors always give you all the information you need to have the trip of a lifetime. Write for your free catalog of all our titles.

Open Road Publishing
P.O. Box 284, Cold Spring Harbor, NY 11724
E-mail: Jopenroad@aol.com

Acknowledgments

English editors: Jonathan Stein and Marian Olson
Maps from designmaps.com
Website (www.eatndrink.com): McDill Design & Susan Chwae
Additional research: Karl Raaum, Mark Berry, Dan Schmidt, Jim Mortell, Jeff Kurz, Jay Filter and Cid Filter
Helpful Dutch Phrases: Math J.H. Geelen, PhD

Text Copyright©2005 by Andy Herbach
ISBN 1-59360-045-3
Library of Congress Control No. 2005925516
–All Rights Reserved–

ABOUT THE AUTHOR

Andy Herbach is the author of Open Road Publishing's *Paris Made Easy* and *Provence Made Easy*, and is the co-author of Open Road's *Eating & Drinking in Paris, Eating & Drinking in Italy, Eating & Drinking in Spain,* and *Eating & Drinking in Latin America.* Look for his forthcoming *Berlin Made Easy.* You can e-mail him corrections, additions, and comments at eatndrink@aol.com or through his website at www.eatndrink.com.

TABLE OF CONTENTS

MAPS

INTRODUCTION

Amsterdam has more canals than Venice, more bridges than Paris, more bicycles than cars, and perhaps more tolerance than any other city in the world. It's what makes Amsterdam truly unique … and such a wonderful place to visit.

Because the city is so compact, you can see a lot even if your stay is short—and its sights are as diverse as its residents, including beautiful churches, lovely gardens, and, of course, the infamous Red-Light District.

If you're interested in museums, there's something for everyone. The famous Rijksmuseum offers paintings from the Dutch Golden Age, the Stedelijk Museum has contemporary art, and the Torture Museum … well, how should we say this? … is filled with stuff you probably didn't need to see!

Cultured, vibrant, fun—and easy to get around—Amsterdam is the perfect European city to explore.

As our title says, this little guide will make your trip to Amsterdam easy. Tuck it into your pocket and head out for a great day of sightseeing: You'll have over 100 places of interest at your fingertips, with insider tips on cafés, restaurants, shops, and outdoor markets. We've also given directions for sight-filled walks around the city, along the canals and, of course, through the "naughty" part of town (this is Amsterdam, after all!).

Forget those large, bulky travel tomes. This handy little pocket guide to Amsterdam is all you need to make your visit enjoyable, memorable— and easy.

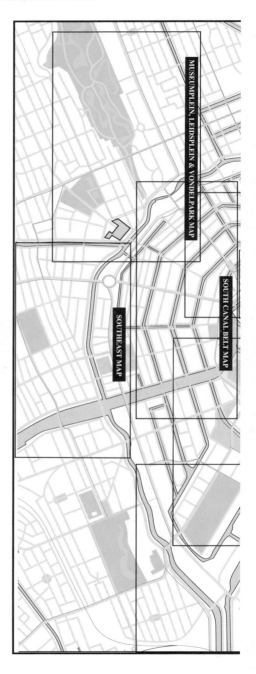

MUSEUMPLEIN, LEIDSPLEIN & VONDELPARK MAP

SOUTH CANAL BELT MAP

SOUTHEAST MAP

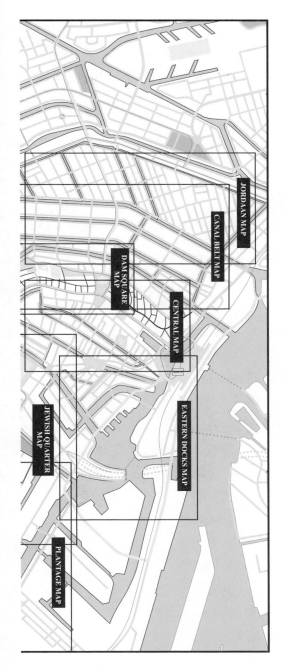

JORDAAN MAP

CANAL BELT MAP

DAM SQUARE MAP

CENTRAL MAP

JEWISH QUARTER MAP

EASTERN DOCKS MAP

PLANTAGE MAP

1. SIGHTS

TOP SIGHTS

Canals: From the Singel to the Prinsengracht, Amsterdam's canals and the Golden Age homes that line them make Amsterdam a unique destination.

Begijnhof: The courtyard of this 14th-century *hofje* (almshouse) is a peaceful getaway from the bustling city.

Anne Frankhuis: Anne Frank's hiding place, where she penned her famous diary, comes to life in this poignant museum.

Rijksmuseum: The Royal Museum is one of the world's greatest art museums with masterpieces by Rembrandt, Vermeer, and countless others.

van Gogh Museum: A study of not only van Gogh's art, but also his fascinating life.

Amsterdams Historisch Museum: Follow the history of Amsterdam from fishing village to modern metropolis.

Red-Light District: The oldest profession in the world sells itself (legally) in a new type of window-shopping.

Museum Amstelkring: Gorgeous clandestine church in, of all places, an attic.

Stedelijk Museum of Modern Art: One of the world's most prestigious modern-art museums.

Coffeeshops: What's that smell? It certainly isn't coffee. Because of Amsterdam's tolerant attitude to certain drugs, you'll find them "served" in the city's numerous coffeeshops.

Central Amsterdam

Centraal Station
(Central Station)

Built in the 1880s in the neo-Renaissance style, the brick façade of this massive train station features scenes of trade and travel. It's the transportation hub of the city, with over 1,500 trains arriving and departing daily. Take a look at all the fascinating destinations on the schedule board.

Restaurant Tip:
Eerste Klas (1e Klas)
Platform 2b in Centraal Station
Tel. 020/625-0131
Open daily 9am-10pm

This beautiful former first-class lounge in Centraal Station will make you forget all those bad cafés and restaurants in other train stations. Even if you don't want to have a meal here, come in, have a drink, and admire the beautiful Art Nouveau interior. Moderate (drinks) to Expensive (dinner).

Stationsplein
In front of Centraal Station

This square is always busy with tourists, locals, street performers, and "entrepreneurs" trying to sell you something. Trams depart from here on the many lines originating at Centraal Station.

Tourist Information Center
(VVV)
10 Stationsplein
Open daily 9am-5pm
www.visitamsterdam.nl

The main tourist information center (VVV) is right outside Centraal Station. The friendly and helpful staff all speak English. They'll assist you with information on public transportation, current events, and day trips. And if you don't have a place to sleep, they'll find one for you for a fee of €3.

Damrak
From Centraal Station to Dam Square

The first street that most travelers to Amsterdam explore is Damrak, the main street connecting Centraal Station and Dam Square. It's filled with fast food outlets and souvenir

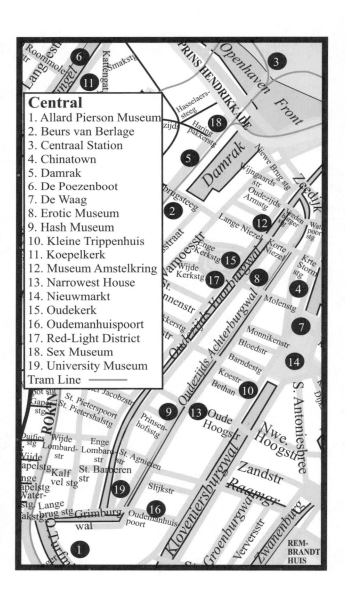

Central

1. Allard Pierson Museum
2. Beurs van Berlage
3. Centraal Station
4. Chinatown
5. Damrak
6. De Poezenboot
7. De Waag
8. Erotic Museum
9. Hash Museum
10. Kleine Trippenhuis
11. Koepelkerk
12. Museum Amstelkring
13. Narrowest House
14. Nieuwmarkt
15. Oudekerk
16. Oudemanhuispoort
17. Red-Light District
18. Sex Museum
19. University Museum
Tram Line ———

shops selling everything from wooden shoes to Dutch chocolate. It's probably Amsterdam's least attractive street. It was a river until 1222 when the Amstel River was dammed, and that's how the city got its name.

XXX

You'll see XXX on places throughout the Red-Light District, and I'm sure you'll know what it means. But you'll also see XXX on the city's coat of arms, flags, and street posts. That's because it's been the symbol of the city for centuries. Saint Andrew, the patron saint of Amsterdam, was crucified on a cross in the shape of an X. Queen Wilhelmina decreed in 1947 that the meaning of XXX would be the virtues of the city: Compassion, resolution, and heroism. Each X is also said to represent, and protect Amsterdam from, three disasters that the city has endured: the plague, floods and fires.

Victoria Hotel
1-5 Damrak at the corner of Prins Hendrikkade

If you take a close look at the façade of this hotel along the street Prins Hendrikkade, you'll see two small 17th-century homes surrounded by the rest of this historic building. It's said that the owners refused to sell their homes so the builder just decided to build around them.

De Poezenboot
(Cat Boat)
40 Singel
Tel. 020/625-8794
Open daily 1pm-3pm
Admission: Donation
www.poezenboot.nl

In 1966, Henriette van Weelde decided to take in a cat and her kittens. Things sort of got out of hand. Henriette kept taking in more and more cats until she couldn't fit all of them in her house. Ultimately, she established a refuge for abandoned and stray cats. The Cat Boat is the only animal sanctuary in the Netherlands that literally floats. It's on a houseboat in the Singel and has become a popular tourist destination. Who said cats don't like water?

Restaurant Tip:

De Silveren Spiegel
4-6 Kattengat
Tel. 020/624-6589
Open daily 6pm-11pm. Lunch
by reservation only
www.desilverenspiegel.com

Admit it: You have a bad impression of Dutch cooking. You'll change your mind after enjoying modern Dutch cooking made with regional products at this elegant and romantic restaurant (the name means "the silver mirror"). It's located in a quaint 1614 building not too far from Centraal Station, next to the domed Koepelkerk. This is Dutch food at its best, including fillet of cod glazed with apple, carrot, leek, and celery purée, and roast suckling pig with gin sauce. There's an interesting story connected to this restaurant: During the Nazi occupation, while SS officers were dining here, the manager hid a family of eleven Jews upstairs. You can still visit the small door leading to the hiding place. Expensive.

Koepelkerk
1 Kattengat
Open for conventions only

This large domed building was a Lutheran church (and the subject of a van Gogh painting). Now it's the convention center for the Renaissance Hotel across the street.

Sex Museum
18 Damrak (near Centraal
Station)
Tel. 020/622-8376
Open daily 10am-11:30pm
Admission: €3
www.sexmuseumamsterdam.com

Eroticism from Greco-Roman times to today, from erotic art to ancient phallic symbols (can you say "dildos"?) to vintage porn films. Just the type of museum you'd expect in this tolerant city.

Tourist Tram
From Prins Hendrikkade
(across from Victoria Hotel)
Tel. 0900/423-1100
Sundays July-Sept noon-4pm
Admission: €5
http://www.museumtram-
amsterdam.nl

This 1920s tram circles the center city in a 50-minute tour.

Beurs van Berlage
(Berlage Stock Exchange)
277 Damrak
(entrance on Beursplein)
Tel. 020/530-4141
Open Tues-Sun 10am-6pm
Admission: €5
www.beursvanberlage.nl

Hendrik Berlage was the father of modern Dutch architecture. This building with its large bell tower was completed in 1903, and housed the Dutch Stock Exchange. Today, it's the home of the Netherlands Philharmonic Orchestra, the Amsterdam Symphony Orchestra, and the Netherlands Chamber Orchestra. Its meeting hall has been used for royal weddings. There's a permanent exhibit on the history of the stock exchange, but the building itself is the real star.

Restaurant Tip:
Beurs van Berlage Café
Beursplein
Tel. 020/638-3914
Open Tues-Sun 10am-6pm

Looking onto the Beursplein, this beautiful café with tile-wall tableaux in the former stock exchange is open for lunch. A great place to enjoy a drink. Moderate.

Museum Amstelkring
(Our Dear Lord in the Attic Museum)
40 Oudezijds Voorburgwal at Heintje Hoeksteeg (on the edge of the Red-Light District)
Tel. 020/624-6604
Open Mon-Sat 10am-5pm, Sun 11am-5pm

Admission: €6
www.museumamstelkring.nl

After the Protestant Reformation, Catholics were forced to worship secretly in clandestine churches. In the mid-1660s, three canal houses were purchased for the purpose of housing a "secret" church. On the ground floor is the merchant's shop and 19th-century kitchen. On the first floor you'll see the formal reception room as it was in the 17th century. The priest's room and the confessional are on the second floor. The highlight is in the attic where you'll be shocked to find a beautiful church complete with pews that can seat 150 people, an 18th-century organ, and an ornate Baroque altar.

Allard Pierson Museum
127 Oude Turfmarkt
Tel. 020/525-2556
Open Tues-Fri 10am-5pm, Sat-Sun 1pm-5pm
Admission: €5
www.uba.uva.nl/apm

This former bank building now houses a collection of archeological finds from Rome, Greece, and Egypt, including statuary, pottery, and mummies.

Zuiderkerk
(South Church)
*72 Zuiderkerkhof (at Sint
Antoniesbreestraat)*
*Tel. 020/622-2962. Tower:
020/689-2565*
*Open Mon 11am-4pm, Tues-
Wed-Fri 9am-4pm, Thurs
9am-8pm*
Admission: Free

This was the first Protestant
church built after the Reformation in the early 1600s. Today, it houses a free exhibit on
the history of urban planning.
The church has a world-famous
carillon (bell tower), which you
can climb for a small price
(guided tours leave on the hour
between June and October,
Wed.-Sun. 2 p.m.-4 p.m.).

SHOPPING TIP

De Klompenboer
*51 Sint
Antoniesbreestraat/20
Nieuwezijds
Voorburgwal
Tel. 020/623-0632
Open Mon 1pm-6pm,
Tues-Wed-Fri 10am-
6pm, Thurs 10am-
9pm, Sat 10am-5pm*

You just have to have a
pair of *klompen* (wooden
shoes), don't you? This
place has a huge selec-
tion.

Nieuwmarkt
(New Market)
*At the north end of
Kloveniersburgwal and the
south end of Geldersekade*

A marketplace since the 15th
century, you can visit the interesting antique market every Sunday during the summer.

Restaurant Tip:
Café Bern
*9 Nieuwmarkt
Tel. 020/622-0034
Open daily 4pm-1am
No credit cards*

The Swiss aren't the only ones
who can properly do fondue.
Here you'll find cheese fondue with a Dutch touch.
They've been serving fondue
and beer here forever. It's not
for everyone, but it sure can be
a fun experience. Inexpensive.

De Waag
(The Waag)
*4 Nieuwmarkt
Tel. 020/557-9898
Open daily
Admission: Depends on the ex-
hibit
www.waag.org*

In the center of Nieuwmarkt is
this former city gate and commercial weigh house (from
which it takes its name). It looks

like a castle and dates back to 1488. Its lively café is in great contrast to its former uses: It was once a prison, the site of public executions, an operating theater for medical students, and, during the Nazi occupation, a processing house for those to be shipped to concentration camps. (It's here that Rembrandt is said to have gotten inspiration for his painting, *The Anatomy Lesson of Dr. Jan Deijman*, now on display in the Amsterdam Historical Museum.) The multimedia center **Waag Society for Old and New Media** is also housed here *(Tel. 020/557-9898).*

Food on the Run Tip:
In de Waag
4 Nieuwmarkt
Tel. 020/422-7772
Open daily 10am-1am
www.indewaag.nl

This café and restaurant in the historic De Waag is a great place to take a break. There's a large selection of reading material (some in English), so you can sip a cup of coffee or glass of wine or beer and catch up on the news or local activities. The café is lively and the restaurant, lit by 300 candles, is quite romantic. Moderate – Expensive (dinner).

Kleine Trippenhuis
(House of Mr. Trip's Coachman)
26 Kloveniersburgwal
Not open to the public

The widest old house in Amsterdam (72 feet) is located at 29 Kloveniersburgwal and now houses the Dutch Academy of Science. It was built in 1660 by the Trip brothers, wealthy merchants and ammunition dealers. Legend has it that the coachman said that he'd be happy with a house as wide as his master's door, so Mr. Trip had this home built for his servant. At less than eight feet wide, it's one of the narrowest houses in the city.

The Narrowest House
22 Oude Hoogstraat
Not open to the public

This house is the narrowest in the city (despite claims by others) and that's saying a lot in this city of narrow houses! Its three-and-one-half stories are only six feet wide and 15 feet long. It's said to have once been a storage area for dead bodies.

Red-Light District

De Walletjes/De Wallen
(Red-Light District)
Behind Dam Square between
Oudezijds Voorburgwal and
Oudezijds Achterburgwal
www.red-light-district.nl

A new spin on window-shopping! Prostitution has been regulated and, of course, taxed in Amsterdam since 1984, and even has its own union. Along the narrow streets of the Red-Light District, women and some men wait in windows for their next customer. The storefront rooms have curtains that are closed when "business" is being conducted. You'll see lots of foreign businessmen and tourists milling around (many very drunk). Be careful at night as the area is a prime pickpocket spot. By the way, don't even think about taking photos. Your camera will likely be confiscated. (Can you believe that it has a web site?)

Chinatown
From the Red-Light District to
Nieuwmarkt (and along
Geldersekade)
Metro to Nieuwmarkt

Amsterdam's "Chinatown" is a misnomer as it's also home to Indonesian, Thai, and Malaysian establishments. Chinatown used to be entirely in the Red-Light District, but today it has expanded to the surrounding area (especially Nieuwmarkt). Ducks hang in the windows of the many Chinese restaurants, and you'll also find many Thai and Indonesian restaurants in the area. The new **Chinese Fo Kuang Shan Buddhist Temple** on Zeedijk can be visited daily from noon-5 p.m. (Sunday 10

SHOPPING TIP

Condomerie Het
Gulden Vlies
141 Warmoesstraat
Tel. 020/627-4174
Open Mon-Sat 11am-
6pm
www.condomerie.nl

What would the Red-Light District be without a condom shop? Hundreds of different kinds of condoms along with lubricants and other "gifts." Only in Amsterdam!

a.m.-5 p.m.) and also has a vegetarian restaurant.

Sex and Amsterdam

From sex clubs to live sex shows (especially the famous **Casa Rosso** at 106 Oudezijds Achterburgwal), sex is a big part of Amsterdam's tourist industry. Locals don't bat an eye at any of this, but you might. If you're not interested in seeing any of it, stay away from the Red-Light District and the area around it. You can easily visit Amsterdam's other wonderful sights without encountering any of the sex industry.

Erotic Museum

54 Oudezijds Achterburgwal
Tel. 020/624-7303
Open Thurs-Mon 11am-1am
(Fri-Sat until 2am)
Admission: €4

It's appropriate that the Erotic Museum is located in the Red-Light District. The history of S&M, porn, sex shows-you get the idea-are on display at this museum. Lots of mannequins doing naughty things. It proudly displays erotic drawings by John Lennon.

Coffeeshops/Smart Shops

Recreational drugs are a big part of Amsterdam's appeal to some tourists. **Coffeeshops** are not cafés. You drink coffee, smoke cigarettes and have a snack at a café. You buy and smoke marijuana at a coffeeshop. How can you tell the difference? Other than the telltale smell, most coffeeshops display a Rastafarian flag (red, yellow and green). Sanctioned shops display a sticker that says "Coffeeshop BCD." Marijuana is sold openly in Amsterdam (although it and all hard drugs remain illegal). About 250 cafés are licensed to sell a maximum of 5 grams per adult. Coffeeshops feature lists of types of marijuana, hashish and *stickie* (a hashish joint rolled with tobacco) from which to choose. It's taxed and regulated. Some shops even have delivery service! They sell cakes, muffins, brownies and chocolates made with hash or marijuana with names like "space cakes" or "space sweets." **Smart Shops** sell hallucinogens (especially "magic mushrooms") and "herbal enhancers" that range from harmless herbal supplements to stimulants that mimic such drugs as Ecstasy. Don't smoke pot on the street as it's considered rude. Never buy drugs from street dealers, and if you choose to partake in the drugs available at these shops, make sure you know what you're getting yourself into. There are many locations of **Bulldog**, said to be the oldest coffeeshop in the city *(www.bulldog.nl)*. Some other coffeeshops around the city include:

•**De Supermarkt**, *69 Frederik Hendrikstraat, www.desupermarkt.net*
•**Grey Area**, *2 Oude Leliestraat, www.greyarea.nl*
•**La Tertulia**, *312 Prinsengracht, www.coffeeshopamsterdam.com*
•**Siberië**, *11 Brouwersgracht, www.siberie.net*

Hash Marihuana Hemp Museum
(Hash Marijuana Hemp Museum)
148 Oudezijds Achterburgwal
Tel. 020/623-5961
Open daily 11am-10pm
Admission: €6
www.hashmuseum.com

Everything you ever wanted to know about cannabis-complete with grow room!

Het KinderKookKafé
(Kids' Café)
193 Oudezijds Achterburgwal
Tel. 020/625-3257
Open Sat 6pm-8pm for dinner, Sun 5pm-6pm for high tea
Admission: €2.50 ages 2-4, €5 ages 5-12, €8 over 12

This cooking school is solely for children. At the café, chil-
dren between the ages of five and twelve try out their culinary skills on customers. Some seats are in the shape of fried eggs, and the artwork is made of colored pasta and candy. If you're over 100, you get to eat free. It's advisable to book ahead as there is often a waiting list.

Oude Kerk
(Old Church)
Oudekerksplein
Tel. 020/625-8284
Open Mon-Sat 11am-5pm, Sun 1pm-5pm
Admission: €5
www.oudekerk.nl

Oude Kerk (Old Church) is exactly that. It's Amsterdam's oldest church. Parts of it date back to the 13th century. Today this Gothic basilica is almost totally surrounded by the Red-Light District. The church is known for its musical concerts. It has a world-famous organ dating back to 1724 and a restored 47-bell carillon. The organ stands on marble pillars that were cleaned and restored in the late 1970s. It's said that you can see the restorer's face in the marble (if you've smoked enough pot) to the left above floor level. Its beautiful stained-glass windows (depicting the death of the Virgin

Mary), decorated pillars, 15th-century carved choir stalls and painted ceiling make this landmark a must for all visitors. There's a great view of the city if you want to climb up the 16th-century bell tower (guided tours). The church is frequently used for exhibitions, and carillon concerts are held frequently.

Oudemanhuispoort
(Old Men's Home Alley)
Between Oudezijds Achterburgwal and Kloveniersburgwal
Once an old men's home, today it's part of the University of Amsterdam. It's Amsterdam's version of *les bouquinistes*, those little green stands along the Seine River in Paris that sell old postcards and books. Here, the covered walkway has small red-shuttered stalls selling ancient (and some not-so-ancient) books.

Food on the Run Tip:
Puccini Bomboni
17 Staalstraat
Tel. 020/626-5474
Open Tues-Sat 9am-6pm, Sun noon-6pm
www.puccinibomboni.com

Calling all chocoholics! You can watch them make fabulous sweets (all made without artificial ingredients) and then buy lots of them to eat.

University Museum
231 Oudezijds Voorburgwal
Tel. 020/525-3339
Open Mon-Fri 9am-5pm
Admission: Free

You can visit the oldest building of the University of Amsterdam and its medieval chapel.

Dam Square

Nationaal Monument
(National Monument)
Dam Square
Admission: Free

The 70-foot obelisk in Dam Square was built in 1956 as a war memorial dedicated to those who endured World War II and the Nazi occupation. Men in chains, snarling dogs and two lions (the symbol of the Netherlands) are all featured on it.

Magna Plaza

182 Nieuwezijds Voorburgwal
(behind Dam Square)
Tel. 020/626-9199
Open Mon 11am-7pm; Tues-
Sat 10am-7pm (Thurs until
9pm); Sun noon-7pm
www.magnaplaza.nl

Built in 1899 and formerly a post office, this incredibly opulent building is now a five-story mall with over 40 stores. Check out the strangely named **Sissy Boy Homeland** store for clothing and interior items.

Koninklijk Paleis

(Royal Palace)
Dam Square/147 Nieuwezijds
Voorburgwal
Tel. 020/640-4060
Open Tues-Sun 12:30pm-
5pm, open daily 11am-5pm
July-Aug
Admission: €5
www.koninklijkhuis.nl

Construction began on this massive palace in the mid-1600s. Originally it served as City Hall, became a royal residence under the rule of Napoleon, and a royal palace of the House of Orange. The royal family doesn't live here anymore, and it's sometimes used for state functions. Its marble-floored **Burgerzaal** (Citizens' Chamber) runs the length of the second floor of the building. You'll find mighty Atlas holding a globe, and maps in the floor portraying Amsterdam as the center of the world. I especially liked the Bankruptcy Office on the north side where there's a sculpture of rats gnawing at unpaid bills.

Madame Tussaud Scenerama

20 Dam Square
Tel. 020/522-1010
Open daily 10am-5pm
Admission: €12

SHOPPING TIP

De Bierkoning

125 Paleisstraat
Tel. 020/625-2336
Open Mon 1pm-7pm,
Tues-Wed-Fri 11am-
7pm, Thurs 11am-
9pm, Sat 11am-6pm,
Sun 1pm-5pm
www.bierkoning.nl

Located near the Royal Palace, the royalty at this small shop is beer (the name means "beer king"). There are nearly 1,000 different brands of beer for sale along with over 300 different glasses. If you like beer, or have a friend back home who loves it, they sell gift packages.

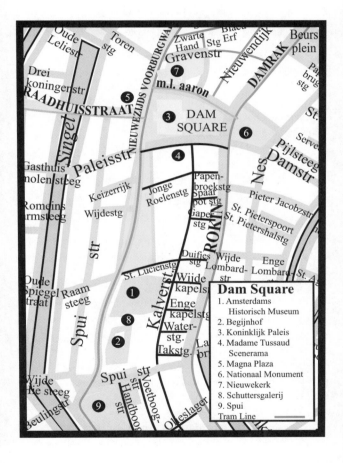

Dam Square
1. Amsterdams Historisch Museum
2. Begijnhof
3. Koninklijk Paleis
4. Madame Tussaud Scenerama
5. Magna Plaza
6. Nationaal Monument
7. Nieuwekerk
8. Schuttersgalerij
9. Spui
Tram Line

Another branch of the famous wax museum.

De Bijenkorf
1 Dam Square
Tel. 0900-0919 or 621-8080
Open Mon 11am-7pm, Tues-Wed 9:30am-7pm, Thurs-Fri 9:30am-9pm, Sat 9:30am-6pm, Sun noon-6pm
www.bijenkorf.nl

Amsterdam's most famous department store overlooks Dam Square and has a large clothing department and a great household-goods section. There are also lots of places to eat.

Albert Heijn
226 Nieuwezijds Voorburgwal
Tel. 020/421 8344
Open Mon-Sat 8am-10pm, Sun 11am-7pm

When you visit a foreign country, you should visit a grocery store to see how different (and sometimes similar) the selection is compared to at home. This branch of the Albert Heijn chain (there are over 40 in the city) is located behind Dam Square. It has long hours, but like most stores here is closed on Sunday mornings. Pick up some inexpensive snacks for your hotel room. One great bargain is the delicious Dutch chocolates sold under the "AH" brand name.

Nieuwe Kerk
(New Church)
Dam Square
Tel. 020/638-6909
Open daily 10am-6pm, closed Jan and Feb
Admission: Free (admission to exhibits)
www.nieuwekerk.nl (current exhibit information)

Dating back to the late 1300s, this Protestant church is, like its name says, newer than the 700-year-old Old Church in the Red-Light District. Today, it's used for state functions and temporary exhibits. Its interior is stark, as this former Catholic church lost most of its decorations and statues during the Iconoclasm of 1566 (when Protestants destroyed the icons, statues, and other decorations of Catholic churches).

Amsterdams Historisch Museum
(Amsterdam Historical Museum)
Three entrances: 92 Kalverstraat, 27 Sint Luciënsteeg and 357 Nieuwezijds Voorburgwal
Tel. 020/523-1822
Open Mon-Fri 10am-5pm, Sat-Sun 11am-5pm

*Admission: €6, €3 ages 6-16,
under 6 free
www.ahm.nl*

This museum, in a former 17th-century orphanage, chronicles the history of Amsterdam from fishing village to modern metropolis. You'll find paintings (including Rembrandt's partly damaged and ghastly *Anatomy Lecture of Dr. Jan Deijman*), maps, wearing apparel, jewelry, prints, porcelain, sculptures, and archeological finds.

The collection is arranged by floor with the "Young City (1350-1550)" on the first floor, the "Mighty City (1550-1815)" on the first and second floors, and the "Modern City (1815-present)" on the second and third floors. One of the highlights of your visit is the huge computerized map on the first floor that tracks Amsterdam's development from 1000 AD. In room 24 (on the third floor) is **Café 't Mandje**, a re-creation of an Amsterdam brown café.

ENTERTAINMENT TIP

*O'Reilly's
103-105 Paleisstraat
Tel. 020/624-9498
Open Sun-Thurs
11am-1am, Fri-Sat
10am-3am
www.oreillys.com*

Many Irish have come to Amsterdam to live and work, and Irish pubs like this one are popular not only with the Irish who are looking for a pint, but also with Amsterdammers. Most Irish pubs feature live music (especially on the weekends). A little bit of Ireland in Amsterdam!

Schuttersgalerij
(Civic Guards Gallery)
In between the courtyard of the Amsterdam Historical Museum and the Begijnhof
*Open Mon-Fri 10am-5pm,
Sat-Sun 11am-5pm
Admission: Free*

This glass-covered passageway is filled with a group of large portraits from the early 1600s of the city's civic guards who initially were responsible for the safety of the city, but later became fraternal groups.

Begijnhof
(Beguine Court)
*Gedempte Begijnensloot at Spui
Courtyard: Open daily 9am-5pm (entry through the gateway at Gedempte Begijnensloot)*

Chapel: Open Mon 1pm-6:30pm, Tues-Fri 9-6:30pm, Sat-Sun 9am-6pm (entry to chapel after 5pm is through the gate off of Spui)
Admission: Free
www.begijnhofamsterdam.nl

There are some 30 *hofjes* (almshouses) throughout Amsterdam. Wealthy merchants in the 18th century established them primarily for the old and poor. Many continue to house the indigent today, so be mindful of their privacy. The courtyard of this 14th-century *hofje* is a peaceful getaway from the bustling city. Founded in 1346 by members of a lay Catholic sisterhood (the Beguines), it's still the home of elderly poor women. There's a statue of a Beguine, dressed in her traditional habit, in the center. You can see the **City's Oldest House** (Het Houten Huis at number 34), the **English Reformed Church** (Engelse Kerk) dating back to the late 1300s, and the **Mother Superior's House** (number 26). The **Begijnhof Chapel** opposite the English Reformed Church houses a clandestine church (like Our Dear Lord of the Attic above).

SHOPPING TIP

Vroom & Dreesmann
203 Kalverstraat
Tel. 020/622-0171
Open Mon 11am-7pm, Tues-Fri 10am-7pm (Thurs until 9pm), Sat 10am-6pm, Sun noon-6pm

This Dutch chain of department stores is popular for its cosmetics and clothing. **La Place**, its cafeteria, serves reasonably priced snacks and salads.

American Book Center
185 Kalverstraat
Tel. 020/625-5534
Open Mon-Tues-Wed-Fri-Sat 10am-8pm, Thurs 10am-9pm, Sun 11am-6:30pm

Great selection of books and magazines from the US, Canada and other English-speaking countries.

BROWN CAFÉS

Amsterdammers love cafés and smoking. A brown café *(bruine kroeg)* gets its name from the brown tobacco stains on the walls.

Spui

Between Singel and Kalverstraat next to the Beguine Court (Begijnhof)

This small square is filled with bookshops, bars and cafés. **Café Hoppe**, a brown café, has been in business for over 300 years. The statue **Little Darling** (*Het Lieverdje*) is of an urchin (the one with hands on hips). On Fridays, there's a book market here, and on Sundays, artists exhibit their works.

Restaurant Tips:
Caffé Esprit
10 Spui
Tel. 020/622-1967
Open daily 10am-6pm (Thurs until 11pm)
No credit cards

Have a hankering for some American food like a burger and fries or delicious pastrami sandwich? This restaurant, owned by the Esprit clothing chain (the one in all those American malls), serves American favorites. The restaurant overlooks the lively Spui square and has an interesting modern industrial design. There's a lively bar with a DJ and dancing at night. Inexpensive - Moderate.

Broodje van Kootje
28 Spui
Tel. 020/623-7451
Open Sun-Thurs 10am-1am, Fri-Sat until 10am-3am

Try a delicious *broodje* (sandwich) at this *broodjeswinkel* (sandwich shop). Aren't those great words! Inexpensive.

Jordaan

Brouwersgracht
(Brewers Canal)
On the northern end of the Singel, Herengracht, Keizersgracht, and Prinsengracht canals

This tree-shaded canal on the north end of the Jordaan neighborhood offers incredibly beautiful views down the four main canals (Prinsengracht, Keizersgracht, Herengracht, and Singel) lined with lovely buildings.

Pianola Museum
(Player Piano Museum)
106 Westerstraat

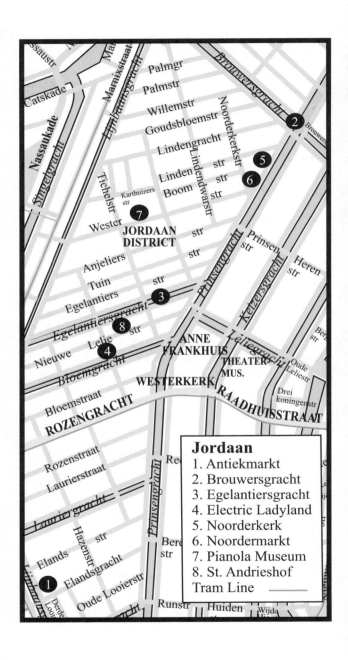

Jordaan
1. Antiekmarkt
2. Brouwersgracht
3. Egelantiersgracht
4. Electric Ladyland
5. Noorderkerk
6. Noordermarkt
7. Pianola Museum
8. St. Andrieshof
Tram Line ———

Tel. 020/627-9624
Open Sun 2pm-5pm
Admission: €5
www.pianola.nl

Talk about a special-interest museum. Everything you wanted to know about the player piano (pianola). Sing-along included in the price of admission.

Antiekmarkt de Looier
(Antique Market)
109 Elandsgracht at Lijnbaansgracht
Tel. 020/624-9038
Open Thurs-Sat 10am-4pm
Admission: Free

This covered market with over 100 stalls offers antiques, art, silverware, furniture, and jewelry from throughout the Netherlands.

Restaurant Tips:
The Jordaan and northern part of the canal belt are home to many great restaurants. There is plenty of diverse cuisine to choose from (Dutch, Italian and Spanish, to name just a few) on Lindengracht alone. Here are a few more:

Seasons
16 Herenstraat
Tel. 020/330-3800
Open Wed-Sat noon-3pm and 6pm-10:30pm, Sun noon-4pm

SHOPPING TIP

Truelove Antique Shop
4 Prinsenstraat
Tel. 020/320-2500
Open daily 11am-6pm
www.truelove.be

The Jordaan is home to many small antique shops where you can find almost anything, if you're willing to dig. One such shop is this one, with a wide variety of antiques and friendly owners.

and 6pm-9:30pm
www.seasonsrestaurant.nl

Friendly restaurant serving international fare and excellent wines. Highly recommended! Moderate.

5 (Vijf)
10 Prinsenstraat
Tel. 020/428-2455
Open Mon-Sat 6pm-10pm
www.bar-restaurant5.nl

Eclectic dining: Dutch with a Mediterranean influence. Try the three- or five-course surprise menu. Moderate.

Restaurant De Belhamel
60 Brouwersgracht

Tel. 020/622-1095
Open daily 6pm-10pm

This restaurant has a beautiful small bar and an excellent reputation. The view down the canal adds to the charm. Moderate - Expensive

Noorderkerk
(North Church)
44-48 Noorderkerk (at Prinsengracht)
Tel. 020/626-6436
Open Mon 10:30am-12:30pm, Sat 11am-1pm, Sun 10am and 7pm for services
Admission: €8
www.noorderkerkconcerten.nl

This early 17th-century church is a premier site for classical concerts held on Thursday evenings and Saturday afternoons.

Noordermarkt
(Northern Market)
Noorderkerkstraat and Westerstraat

An organic farmers' market (with an occasional medieval music festival) is held Saturdays 10 a.m.-4 p.m. around the Noorderkerk, along with a bird market. There's also a popular flea market Mondays 9am-1pm.

Restaurant Tips:
Bordewijk
7 Noordermarkt
Tel. 020/624-3899
Open Tues-Sun 6:30pm-10:30pm

French (and some Italian) cuisine at this fun, funky, and bustling restaurant with modern décor. Great wine list. You'll need reservations. Moderate - Expensive.

Proust
4 Noordermarkt
Tel. 020/623-9145
Open daily noon-10pm (Mon and Sat from 9am)

Friendly, informal bar and restaurant serving simple pasta dishes, beef dishes, great hamburgers and fantastic french fries. Inexpensive - Moderate.

Egelantiersgracht
A canal running west of Prinsengracht

Once a drainage ditch, it was converted into a lovely canal in the 17th century. It's a great place for a tree-lined stroll.

Electric Ladyland
5 Tweede Leliedwarsstraat
(off the Prinsengracht, between the Bloemgracht and the Egelantiersgracht)
Tel. 030/420-3776

Open Tues-Sun 1pm-6pm
Admission: €5
www.electric-lady-land.com

The "First Museum of Fluorescent Art" is located downstairs from the Electric Lady Art Gallery. What a trip! Part of the museum is a large "fluorescent environment," where you become part of the art (especially, one can presume, if you've visited a coffeeshop first). The other part features displays of fluorescent artifacts and advertisements dating back to 1938.

Food on the Run Tip:
Café 't Smalle
12 Egelantiersgracht

Tel. 020/623-9617
Open daily 10am-1am (Fri-Sat until 2am)

A former distillery, this café has been open since 1786. Outdoor terrace along the water. Moderate.

St. Andrieshofje
107-114 Egelantiersgracht
Open daily (times vary)

The courtyard of this serene *hofje* (almshouse) dating back to the 1600s is reached through a passageway lined with attractive blue-and-white tiles. Don't be afraid to open the door to enter, although sometimes it's locked.

Canal Belt

Negen Straatjes
(Nine Streets)
Nine streets between Leidsegracht and Raadhuisstraat
These nine small streets near the Royal Palace are loaded with specialty shops, a nice break from department and chain stores found in other parts of the city. For the ultimate in specialty shops, visit my favorite, **De Witte Tanden Winkel**, *5 Runstraat, Tel. 020/*

623-3443. It has a huge selection of toothbrushes and toothpaste of every imaginable flavor! For period clothing (mostly from the 1940s and 1950s), try **Laura Dols**, *6-7 Wolvenstraat, Tel. 020/624-9066.*

Restaurant Tip:
Lust
13 Runstraat
Tel. 020/626-5791

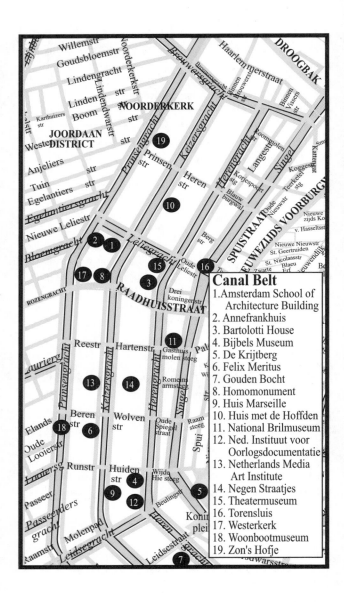

Canal Belt

1. Amsterdam School of Architecture Building
2. Annefrankhuis
3. Bartolotti House
4. Bijbels Museum
5. De Krijtberg
6. Felix Meritus
7. Gouden Bocht
8. Homomonument
9. Huis Marseille
10. Huis met de Hoffden
11. National Brilmuseum
12. Ned. Instituut voor Oorlogsdocumentatie
13. Netherlands Media Art Institute
14. Negen Straatjes
15. Theatermuseum
16. Torensluis
17. Westerkerk
18. Woonbootmuseum
19. Zon's Hofje

Open daily 9:30am-11pm
www.lustamsterdam.nl

Great place for lunch while shopping in the Nine Streets. Pasta dishes, salads, and stir-fry dishes. Check out the bathrooms (seriously)! Inexpensive.

Nationaal
Brilmuseum
(*National Eyeglass Museum*)
7 Gasthuismolensteeg
Tel. 020/421-2414
Open Wed-Fri noon-5:30pm,
Sat noon-5pm
Admission: €5
www.brilmuseumamsterdam.nl

Everything you cared to know about eyeglasses, from Schubert's to some shaped like diamonds. The museum is located in chambers dating back to 1620.

ENTERTAINMENT TIP

De Twee Zwaantjes
114 Prinsengracht
Tel. 020/625-2729
Open Thurs-Tues
3pm-1am (Fri-Sat
until 3am)
www.detweezwaantjes.nl

You can hear folk singers on Sunday afternoons at this popular brown café.

Restaurant Tip:
Bolhoed
60-62 Prinsengracht
Tel. 020/626-1803
Open daily noon-10pm (Sat until 11pm)

Want to eat healthy? This vegetarian restaurant serves dishes made with organic ingredients. Very funky and very "granola." Inexpensive.

Zon's Hofje
159-171 Prinsengracht
Open Mon-Fri 10am-6pm

Another lovely *hofje* (almshouse), and once the site of a "secret" church. Noah's Ark is on the stone wall plaque. (Street numbers weren't used until 1795. Before this, buildings were identified by wall plaques. They frequently identified not only the house, but also the religion, occupation, or origin of the owner.) Don't be afraid to open the door, walk through the dark hall, and duck into the small courtyard.

Restaurant Tip:
Pancake Bakery
191 Prinsengracht
Tel. 020/625-1333
Open daily noon-9:30pm
www.pancake.nl

The Dutch love their pancakes and this is the best place

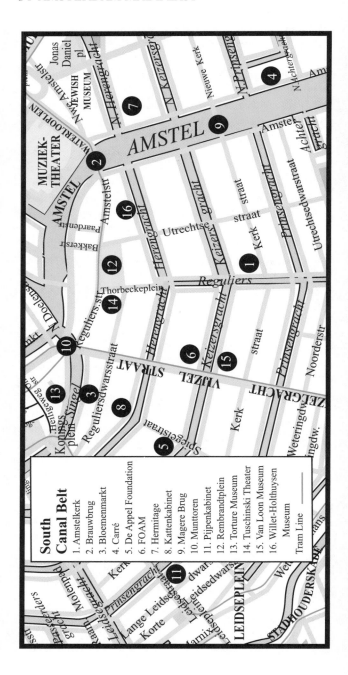

South Canal Belt

1. Amstelkerk
2. Brauwbrug
3. Bloemenmarkt
4. Carré
5. De Appel Foundation
6. FOAM
7. Hermitage
8. Kattenkabinet
9. Magere Brug
10. Munttoren
11. Pijpenkabinet
12. Rembrandtplein
13. Torture Museum
14. Tuschinski Theater
15. Van Loon Museum
16. Willet-Holthuysen Museum

— Tram Line

to try them, the most famous Dutch pancake (and omelet) restaurant in Amsterdam. It's housed in an old 17th-century warehouse near the Anne Frank House. There's an incredible choice of toppings, from cheese and pineapple to raisins and cheese. Great menu for kids, with pancakes in the shape of things like police officers or clowns. Inexpensive.

SHOPPING TIP

Simon Levelt Koffie & Thee
180 Prinsengracht
Tel. 020/624-0823
Open Mon-Fri 10am-6pm, Sat 10am-5pm
www.simonlevelt.com

Experiencing a little jet lag? Buy some of the great coffee and tea found here. Several other locations throughout the city. Inexpensive.

Westerkerk
(West Church)
281 Prinsengracht
Tel. 020/624-7766
Open Apr-Sept, Mon-Fri 11am-3pm; Sun 10:30am for services
Admission: Free. €3 to the tower
www.westerkerk.nl

Hendrick de Keyser, a popular Dutch architect of the Golden Age, designed this Protestant church with its landmark tower. Completed in 1631, its ornate organ is in stark contrast to its unadorned interior. Rembrandt is buried here–in a pauper's grave–so the location is unknown.

Homomonument
(Homosexual Monument)
Next to the Westerkerk Church
Open at all times
Admission: Free
www.homomonument.info

Homosexuals were rounded up by the Nazis during World War II, forced to wear pink triangles, and sent to concentration camps. Dedicated in 1987, the monument, made of three pink granite triangles, points toward the Anne Frank House. Since Amsterdam is known for its tolerance, it's appropriate that it's home to the first monument of its kind in the world. Nearby is **Pink Point**, a gay tourist information booth.

Gay Amsterdam
www.gayamsterdam.com (information)

Gays and lesbians have long had equal rights in the Netherlands, and same-sex marriage has been legal here since 2001. The city is a huge destination for gay and lesbian travelers, especially during Gay Pride Parade held the first week in August. There are many gay hotels, bed and breakfasts, restaurants, and bars. Some bars around the city are listed below:

April, *20 Reguliersdwarsstraat, www.april-exit.com*
Exit, *42 Reguliersdwarsstraat, www.april-exit.com*
Queen's Head, *20 Zeedijk, www.queenshead.nl*
Barderij, *14 Zeedijk*

Anne Frankhuis
(Anne Frank House)
263 Prinsengracht
Tel. 020/556-7100
Open daily 9am-7pm, closed Jewish holidays
Admission: €8, €4 ages 10-17, under 10 free
www.annefrank.nl

The Diary of Anne Frank has been published in over 60 languages; has sold well over ten million copies; and tells the story of a Jewish teenager, her sister, parents, and friends who lived in hiding from the Nazis for two years before being discovered and sent to a concentration camp. Only Anne's father Otto survived. Anne's hiding place within the re-

SHOPPING TIPS

BLGK Edelsmeden
28 Hartenstraat
Tel. 020/624-8154
Open Mon-Fri 11am-6pm, Sat 11am-5pm

You'll find interesting and affordable jewelry at this shop run by jewelry designers.

't Winkeltje
228 Prinsengracht
Tel. 020/625-1352
Open Mon 1pm-5:30pm, Tues-Fri 10am-5:30pm, Sat 10am-5pm

Lots of weird stuff, from glassware to mechanical children's toys.

stored home is one of the most visited sites in Amsterdam. The movable bookcase through which the family entered and the cramped attic rooms bring her diary–on display here–to life. There's also an annex for exhibitions on anti-Semitism, a souvenir shop, and a café. The tour is quite poignant. You see Anne as the teenager she was, even down to the pictures of movie stars that she had pinned to her wall. When I visited the first time, I was moved to tears. There's almost always a line to gain entrance.

Woonbootmuseum
(Houseboat Museum)
Docked opposite
296 Prinsengracht
Tel. 020/427-0750
Open Mar-Oct Tues-Sun 11am-5pm, Nov-Feb Fri-Sun 11am-5pm
Admission: €3
www.houseboatmuseum.nl

Over 2,500 houseboats are home to Amsterdammers. They became particularly popular during the 1950s when there was a housing shortage. The Houseboat Museum is located on a 1914 barge that was converted into a houseboat before becoming the museum.

Pijpenkabinet
(Pipe Cabinet)
488 Prinsengracht
Tel. 020/421-1779
Open Wed-Sat noon-6pm
Admission: €5
www.pijpenkabinet.nl

The Dutch are big smokers, so it's not surprising that you'd find an entire museum (and shop) devoted to pipe smoking. Over 2,000 pipes from ancient times to today–including the world's largest clay pipe–are displayed in 20 display cases.

SHOPPING TIP

Frozen Fountain
645 Prinsengracht
Tel. 020/622-9375
Open Mon 1pm-6pm, Tues-Fri 10am-6pm, Sat 10am-5pm
www.frozenfountain.nl

Home furnishings (some that are totally bizarre) and household goods from Dutch and international designers.

Restaurant Tip:
Le Zinc et Les Autres
999 Prinsengracht
Tel. 020/622-9044
Open Tues-Sun 5:30pm-11pm

Le Zinc, named after the antique zinc bar that originated in Paris, is located on two floors of a beautifully restored warehouse with a French and Mediterranean country motif. You'll enjoy French cuisine at reasonable prices, and there's a great wine list at the bar. Moderate.

Huis met de Hoofden
(House With the Heads)

123 Keizersgracht
Not open to the public

This mansion, built in the 1620s, gets its name from the six heads featured on its elaborate exterior. They're said to portray the deities Apollo, Ceres, Mars, Minerva, Diana, and Bacchus–but legend has it that they really represent burglars who had their heads chopped off by a maid!

Amsterdam School of Architecture
176 Keizersgracht
Not open to the public

This "modern" building is an excellent example of the Amsterdam school of architecture. It's the former headquarters of the environmental group Greenpeace.

Netherlands Media Art Institute
264 Keizersgracht
Tel. 020/623-7101
Open Mon-Fri 9am-5pm (gallery open Tues-Sat 1pm-6pm)
Admission: Depends on the exhibit
www.montivideo.nl

This institute is dedicated to media art and has a gallery with changing exhibits.

Felix Meritis Building
324 Keizersgracht
Tel. 020/623-1311
Open for events only
Admission: Depends on the event
www.felix.meritis.nl

This impressive neo-Classical building, built in 1787, was the home of a society of wealthy residents of Amsterdam called the Felix Meritis Society, which means "happiness through merit." The society survives today and is dedicated to connecting the world's cultures. Its opulent theater–the Shaffy Theater– has excellent acoustics and still hosts performances.

Huis Marseille
401 Keizersgracht
Tel. 020/531-8989
Open Tues-Sat 11am-5pm
Admission: €3
www.huismarseille.nl

Huis Marseille, the Foundation for Photography, opened in 1999. The stone tablet on the façade features a plan of the city of Marseille, France, and dates back to 1665 when the canal house was built by a wealthy French merchant. The interesting photography exhibits here change every three months.

Restaurant Tip:

Walem
449 Keizersgracht
Tel. 020/625-3544
Open daily 11am-10:30pm

Enjoy eclectic dishes at this trendy café with dining along the canal. A great place for breakfast and good salads at lunch. Inexpensive – Moderate.

De Appel Foundation
10 Nieuwe Spiegelstraat
Tel. 020/625-5651
Open Tues-Sun 11am-6pm
Admission: €5
www.deappel.nl
Contemporary art center with changing exhibits.

FOAM Museum for Photography
609 Keizersgracht
Tel. 020/551-6500
Open daily 10am-5pm (Thurs-Fri until 9pm)
Admission: €5
www.foam.nl

Historical and contemporary photography by both established artists and emerging young talent. A must for photography buffs.

Van Loon Museum
672 Keizersgracht (near Vijzelstraat)
Tel. 020/624-5255

SHOPPING TIPS

Metz & Co
455 Keizersgracht
Tel. 020/520-7020 or is it 7048
Open Mon-Sat 9:30am-6pm, Sun noon-5pm

This is Amsterdam's upscale department store. Lots of luxury household goods and designer clothes. The highlight here is the penthouse café (**M'Café**) with great views.

Art Multiples
510 Keizersgracht
Tel. 020/624-8419
Open Mon-Sat 10am-6pm, Sun noon-5pm
www.artmultiples.nl

This gift shop specializes in art posters and postcards. In fact, there are postcards here of every imaginable kind. It's the kind of store you can spend way too much time in.

Open Fri-Mon 11am-5pm
Admission: €5

When the Eighty Years' War ended in 1648, the Dutch expelled the Spanish and established an independent state. This began the Golden Age. Merchants amassed fortunes, and art and culture flourished. You can return to this extraordinary time in this old canal house built in 1672, which was inhabited by the van Loon family from 1884 to 1945. The mansion contains furnishings and art, and there's a lovely rose garden. There are also portraits of the families who called this their home over the years. Some highlights are the remarkable staircase with brass banisters, the dining room with its collection of porcelain dishes, the red drawing room/smoking room with its gold coin collection, the lovely garden room, the painted room with elaborately painted wallpaper, and the coach house at the end of the garden.

Gables
206-210 Kerkstraat
Not open to the public

Look up at the roofs on most buildings in Amsterdam, and you'll likely find the gables that the city is famous for, from the simple point to the triangular step. Here, on Kerkstraat, you'll see some interesting modern variations on the old themes. Yes, those are car tires!

Theatermuseum
(Theater Museum)
168 Herengracht (at Leliegracht)
Tel. 020/551-3300
Open Mon-Fri 11am-5pm, Sat-Sun 1pm-5pm
Admission: €5 (includes Bartolotti House below)
www.tin.nl

These two beautiful and ornate canal houses, complete with period garden, are the home to a museum showcasing the performance arts, everything from puppets to opera costumes to set designs. Check out the miniature theater dating back to 1781. But if you ask me, the buildings are the real stars.

Bartolotti House
170-172 Herengracht
Tel. 020/551-3300
Open Mon-Fri 11am-5pm, Sat-Sun 1pm-5pm
Admission: Included in the price of the Theatermuseum

Built in 1617, you can't miss the Dutch Renaissance façade and the red brick gable of the Bartolotti House. The interior is richly decorated, especially the stucco decorations in the corridor and the painted ceilings.

Bijbels Museum
(Biblical Museum)

366-368 Herengracht (at
Huidenstraat)
Tel. 020/624-2436
Open Mon-Sat 10am-5pm,
Sun 11am-5pm
Admission: €6
www.bijbelsmuseum.nl

Two 17th-century buildings are home to this museum aimed at bringing Bible stories to life. It's packed with archeological finds, religious objects, centuries-old models of historical religious sites, and artifacts from ancient Egypt and the Middle East.

Restaurant Tip:
Pianeta Terra
7 Beulingstraat
Tel. 020/6261912
Open daily 6pm-10:30pm (Fri-Sat until 11pm)
www.pianetaterra.nl

This wonderful restaurant is hidden on a small street between the Singel and Herengracht. It serves Mediterranean and Italian dishes, many with organic ingredients. A good choice for vegetarians as the menu often offers meatless dishes. Moderate – Expensive.

Nederlands Instituut
voor Oorlogsdocumentatie
(Netherlands Institute for War Documentation)
380 Herengracht

Tel. 020/523-3800
Open Mon-Fri 9am-5pm
Admission: Free
www.niod.nl

This institute, with an extensive library and archives of over 100,000 photos, is dedicated to chronicling the occupation of the Netherlands during World War II and the Japanese occupation of the Dutch East Indies. There are occasional exhibits here, but the real star is the fantastic castle-like exterior with sculptures of mythical figures.

Restaurant Tip:
Zuid Zeeland
413 Herengracht
Tel. 020/624-3154
Open Mon-Fri noon-2:30pm for lunch, daily 6pm-11pm for dinner
www.zuidzeeland.nl

This bustling restaurant with contemporary décor serves straightforward international fare. Its menu features a delicious and interesting deer tenderloin, and an extensive wine list. Expensive.

Gouden Bocht
(Golden Bend)
Herengracht between Leidsestraat and Vijzelstraat

It was here that the bigwigs

built their homes in the 17th and 18th centuries. They remain today for you to appreciate. Two especially stand out (numbers 475 and 527), both in the over-the-top Louis XVI style.

Kattenkabinet
(Cat Cabinet)
497 Herengracht
Tel. 020/626-5378
Open Mon-Fri 10am-2pm, Sat-Sun 1pm-5pm
Admission: €5
www.kattenkabinet.nl

Calling all cat lovers! This is the only museum in the world to feature a collection of paintings and other art objects devoted solely to cats. From Egyptian bronze statues to *Le Chat* by Picasso, you'll certainly get your fill of kitties!

Willet-Holthuysen Museum
605 Herengracht
(at Utrechtsestraat)
Tel. 020/523-1822
Open Mon-Fri 10am-5pm, Sat-Sun 11am-5pm
Admission: €4, €2 ages 6-15, under 6 free
www.willetholthuysen.nl

This restored canal house dates back to 1687. Its last residents were Abraham Willet and his wife Louisa Holthuysen (who died in 1895). She left the house with its contents and her husband's sizeable art collection to the city on the condition that the house become a museum. There are many period rooms loaded with tapestries, Delft china, portraits, and a lot of stuff that must take a long time to dust.

Blauwbrug
(Blue Bridge)
On the Amstel River

It's believed that this bridge got its name from the blue color of the 17th-century bridge that was originally at this site. The lovely stone bridge you see today was constructed in 1883 for the World Exhibition, and stone carvings of maritime themes and beautiful lamps are its main features.

Restaurant Tips:
Keuken van 1870
4 Spuistraat
Tel. 020/620-4018
Open Mon-Sat 4pm-10:30pm

Traditional Dutch dishes such as *stamppot* (sausage, potato and vegetable stew) served in a former soup kitchen. There's nothing (and I mean nothing) spicy here. A perfect place for comfort food on a cold and rainy day. You'll share a table with others, which is a great way to meet locals and other travelers. Inexpensive.

Café Luxembourg
24 Spuistraat
Tel. 020/620-6264
Open Sun-Thurs 9am-1am
(Fri-Sat until 2am)

An eclectic menu, an interesting crowd, and one of the most beautiful interiors in all of Amsterdam make this a great place for a bite and a drink. Inexpensive.

Green Planet
122 Spuistraat
Tel. 020/625-8280
Open Tues-Sun 5:30pm-midnight
No credit cards
www.greenplanet.nl

Inexpensive dishes made with organic ingredients at this popular vegetarian restaurant. Inexpensive.

Kantjil en de Tijger
291-293 Spuistraat
Tel. 020/620-0994
Open daily 4:30pm-11pm
www.kantjil.nl (in Dutch)

This lively and large restaurant with a classic modern interior serves *rijsttafel* (a rice table with many dishes of vegetables, fish and meat along with sauces from mild to un-believably hot) and other Indonesian dishes. Lots of groups sharing dishes. Moderate – Expensive.

D' Vijff Vlieghen
294-302 Spuistraat
Tel. 020/530-4060
Open daily at 5:30pm
www.d-vijffvlieghen.com

The name of this unpronounceable restaurant means "five flies." It's located in five beautiful buildings. Excellent Dutch cuisine with an emphasis on exotic recipes featuring herbs and spices discovered by Dutch explorers

SHOPPING TIP

Maison de Bonneterie
140-142 Rokin
Tel.020/531-3400
Open Mon 1pm-5:30pm; Tues-Sat 10am-5:30pm (Thurs until 9pm), Sun noon-5pm
www.debonneterie.nl (in Dutch)

This department store with beautiful chandeliers and a glass dome is known for its men's and women's fashions and household goods. It's been in business since 1889.

in their former colonies. Most of the ingredients are organically grown. Incredible wine list. You'll need reservations, a jacket and tie, and a large wallet. Very Expensive.

Torensluis
(Towers Bridge)
On the Singel canal between Torensteeg and Oude Leliestraat

This bridge was once the site where local authorities locked up drunks. One of the widest bridges along the canals (the extra space accommodated a tower demolished in 1828), it's filled with cafés (go ahead, have a drink!) offering great views of the Singel canal.

De Krijtberg
446 Singel
Tel. 020/623-1923
Open daily. Sunday services are held in Latin (9:30am), Dutch (12:30pm and 5:15pm) and feature Gregorian chant (11am)
Admission: Free
www.krijtberg.nl

You can't miss the two steeples of this 1880s neo-Gothic church. The name means "chalk church" since the church was built on the site of a home owned by a chalk merchant. Its real name is St. Francis Xavier Church

(Franciscus Xaveriuskerk). Head inside to take a look at the rich interior illuminated by colorful stained-glass windows. The statue of St. Francis Xavier is to the left of the altar, the detailed wood carving of the Immaculate Conception is near the pulpit, and the statue of St. Ignatius (the founder of the Jesuits) is to the right of the altar.

Torture Museum
449 Singel
Tel. 020/320-6642
Open daily 10am-11pm
Admission: €5
www.torturemuseum.com

Yikes! The things they did to punish people in the past. This museum (you enter through a long, dark tunnel) has all the things you're thankful that you've never had to face: guillotine, Inquisition chair, iron maidens, chair of spikes, hot iron rods … you get the picture. Makes you want to run out and contribute to Amnesty International. Did I really need to see this?

Reflex Miniatuur Museum voor Hedendaagse Kunst
(Reflex Miniature Museum)
548 Singel (in the Fortis Bank Building)
Tel. 020/627-2832 (for information)

Open Mon 1pm-5pm, Tues-Fri 9:30am-5pm
Admission: Free
www.reflex-art.nl

This self-proclaimed world's smallest museum has works from such notables as Christo, Botero, Leibovitz, and Picasso. Its collection contains over 1,500 miniature sculptures, paintings, and drawings.

Bloemenmarkt
(Flower Market)
Singel between Koningsplein and Muntplein
Open Mon-Fri 9am-6pm, Sat 9am-5pm
Admission: Free

Stalls selling cut flowers and bulbs are sold from "floating" anchored barges on the Singel Canal. It's incredibly fragrant and a great photo opportunity. Don't miss a walk though this beautiful sight. It's the only floating flower market in the world.

Munttoren
(Mint Tower)
Muntplein
Gift shop closed Sun
Admission: Free

In medieval times, this tower was part of a gate in the city walls. When the gate burned down in 1690, the clock tower and steeple were added. The tower gets its name from the time when it was used as a mint during the French occupation of the city in the 1600s. There's a souvenir shop on the ground floor, but the rest of the tower is closed to the public. The bells ring every 15 minutes.

Tuschinski Cinema
26-28 Reguliersbreestraat
Tel. 020/626-2633
Open: Movie schedule varies
www.pathe.nl (in Dutch)

Opened in 1921 and recently renovated, this over-the-top Art Deco masterpiece complete with Wurlitzer organ still shows movies from silent films to new releases. Tuschinski was a Jewish immigrant from Poland who wanted to create a theater where everyone could feel like a king or queen. He succeeded. Today, you can rent a box and sip champagne while watching a film. You can also watch a film at the nearby **Tuschinski Arthouse**, *34 Reguliersbreestraat.*

Restaurant Tip:
Tempo Doeloe
75 Utrechtsestraat
Tel. 020/625-6718
Open daily 6pm-11:30pm
Reservations required
www.tempodoeloerestaurant.nl

Indonesia was a Dutch colony until 1949 so you'll find many Indonesian restaurants in Amsterdam. This is one of the best places to try *rijsttafel* (a rice table with many dishes of vegetables, fish and meat along with sauces from mild to unbelievably hot). There are also lots of vegetarian dishes and specialties such as *gadon dari sapi* (beef in a creamy coconut sauce with fresh coriander). It's always crowded, so make reservations. At 73 Utrechtsestraat is the less formal and cheaper **Tujuh Maret** *(Tel. 020/427-9865)*. Inexpensive (Tujuh Maret) Moderate – Expensive (Tempo Doeloe).

Hermitage Amsterdam
14 Nieuwe Herengracht
Tel. 020/530-8751
Open daily 10am-5pm
Admission: €6, under 17 free
www.hermitage.nl/en

Opened in 2004, The Hermitage Amsterdam exhibits works on loan from the famous Hermitage collection in Saint Petersburg (Russia's pre-eminent art museum). The museum is housed in the "Amstelhof," a former old-age home on the Amstel River.

Rembrandtplein
(Rembrandt Square)
Adjacent to Thorbeckeplein.

Between Herengracht and Amstelstraat

A statue of Rembrandt was placed in this square in 1876. It used to be called "Botermarkt" after the butter market that was held here. Today, it's a lively square filled with outdoor cafés. One of them is **De Kroon** at number 17. You'll know it when you see its waiters in long white aprons serving customers beneath crystal chandeliers.

Magere Brug
(Skinny Bridge)
Over the Amstel River between Keizersgracht and Nieuwe Keizersgracht and Prinsengracht and Nieuwe Prinsengracht

Some say this bridge was built in the 17th century by the Magere sisters who lived across the Amstel River from each other and were too lazy to walk far to visit. Others say the bridge got its name from the word *mager* (which means skinny or narrow). Either way, it's a great photo opportunity. Built in the traditional Dutch drawbridge style, it's raised frequently to allow boats to pass. The bridge that's in place today was constructed in 1969. (It's really not that skinny.)

Amstelkerk

10 Amstelveld (corner of Reguliersgracht and Prinsengracht)
Tel. 020/627-0245
Open weekdays and Sun for services
Admission: Free (admission charged to concerts)

Built in the late 1600s as a temporary place of worship, this white wooden church was renovated in the mid-1800s in the Gothic style. Today it houses offices, a restaurant, and café. You can still step inside and admire the church, which is the site of frequent classical music concerts.

Carré

115-125 Amstel
Tel. 0900/252-5255 (events)

GO TO A CONCERT!

You'll see posters all over advertising choral or orchestra concerts, sometimes at bargain prices. Usually, these concerts are held in less-known churches throughout Amsterdam and make for a wonderful evening before or after dinner.

Open for events only
www.theatercarre.nl

This large building on the Amstel River was originally built in 1894 as a circus theater. Today, it features everything from circus acts to opera.

Museumplein & Vondelpark

Rijksmuseum

(Royal Museum)
1 Jan Luijkenstraat
(along Stadhouderskade)
Open daily 9am-6pm
Tel. 020/674-7000 or 670-7047
Admission: €9, under 19 free
www.rijksmuseum.nl
Trams: 2 and 5 (to Hobbemastraat)

Opened in 1800 as the Nationale Konstgallerij, the Rijksmuseum is known for its rich decoration, impressive galleries and gardens.

A long-planned and very lengthy renovation is underway until 2008. Some of the art is now on display at the airport and other locations throughout the Netherlands.

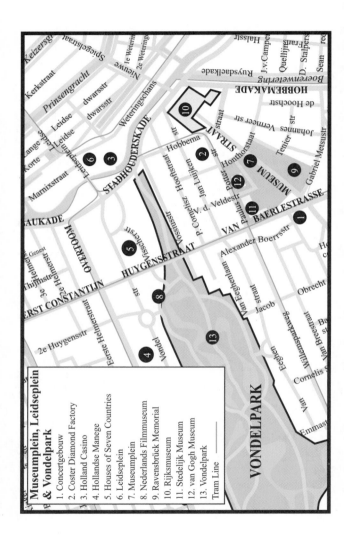

Museumplein, Leidseplein & Vondelpark

1. Concertgebouw
2. Coster Diamond Factory
3. Holland Casino
4. Hollandse Manege
5. Houses of Seven Countries
6. Leidseplein
7. Museumplein
8. Nederlands Filmmuseum
9. Ravensbrück Memorial
10. Rijksmuseum
11. Stedelijk Museum
12. van Gogh Museum
13. Vondelpark

Tram Line ———

During the renovation, the museum is featuring an exhibit, "The Masterpieces," in the renovated Philips Wing of the museum. More than 400 highlights from the Dutch Golden Age are on display, including:

• *The Night Watch*, Rembrandt's best known and largest canvas;
• *Portrait of Two Figures From the Old Testament* by Rembrandt;
• *The Kitchen Maid* by Johannes Vermeer;
• *The Mill at Wijk Bij Duurstede* by Jacob van Ruisdael (one of the most famous 17th-century Dutch landscape painters);
• *Doll's House of Petronella Oortman* (a marvelous example of a 17th-century doll's house collected by wealthy women);
• *Flower Pyramid*, a 17th-century Delft vase from the museum's extensive collection of Delft porcelain. It's over three feet tall.

When the museum reopens it will feature the following collections, some of which will be displayed during the renovation in the Philips Wing:

• A huge collection of European paintings (especially Spanish works);
• Dutch paintings from the middle ages to today (there's an incredible collection of 17th-century paintings and, of course, a self-portrait by van Gogh);
• Artifacts tracing Dutch history and exploration;
• A large sculpture collection;
• Textiles and costumes from the 18th and 19th centuries;
• A collection of decorative arts, especially Delftware (Dutch handpainted blue-and-white china);
• A collection of Asian art (especially Indonesian) comprised of items mostly obtained during the Netherlands's colonial times.

Behind the museum is an interesting garden that's often overlooked by visitors. Among the fountains and flowers is a display of the ruins of buildings, some dating back to the 17th century, from throughout the Netherlands. Admission to the garden is free.

Museumplein
(Museum Square)
Stretching from the back of the Rijksmuseum to the Concertgebouw

This is the city's largest square, used for everything from political demonstrations to picnics. You'll find lots of green grass, a children's playground, and a pond that's an ice-skating rink in the winter.

Ravensbruckmonument
(Ravensbrück Memorial)
Museumplein
Open at all times
Admission: Free

Built in 1975, this interesting war memorial is dedicated to the women who were prisoners in the Ravensbrück concentration camp in Germany from 1939 to 1945. It features a stainless-steel column that incorporates lights and menacing sounds. Unfortunately, it sometimes sounds like the batteries are running low. With your back to the Rijksmuseum, it's located in the far left corner of the Museumplein.

Concertgebouw
2-6 Concertgebouwplein
Tel. 020/671-8345 (box office)
020/573-0511 (information)
Open for concerts
Admission depends on the event
www.concertgebouw.nl

This beautiful concert hall with a columned neo-Classical façade was built in 1888, and is said to have some of the best acoustics in the world. It's the home of the Royal Concertgebouw Orchestra, and features concerts by many of the world's best orchestras.

Food on the Run Tip:
Van Altena
Stadhouderskade (across from the Rijksmuseum)
Tel. 020/676-9139
Open Tues-Sun 11am-7pm
No credit cards

The Dutch love the sea and seafood. They love herring and love to eat it raw. It's definitely an acquired taste! This is the city's best-known and most popular herring stand. It's run by its funny and friendly owner. If you just can't deal with raw or pickled herring or smoked eel, they also serve other kinds of fish and seafood salads. Inexpensive.

Stedelijk Museum of Modern Art
13 Paulus Potterstraat (closed for renovation)
Currently located in a temporary space in the Eastern Docks area at 5 Oosterdokskade near Centraal Station
Tel. 020/573-2911/020/573-2737 (information)
Open daily 10am-6pm (Thurs until 9pm)
Admission: €9
www.stedelijkmuseum.nl (in Dutch)

When you think of art in Amsterdam, you think about all those Rembrandts. Maybe you need to look at some modern art! This museum, one of the world's most prestigious modern-art museums, is housed in a neo-Renaissance building constructed in 1895. Inside, you'll find works by Manet, Monet, Picasso, Pollock, Warhol, Chagall, and Cézanne. You'll also find pieces by many Dutch artists such as Appel and Mondrain. From paintings to video to photography, this museum features an impressive display of contemporary works.

Restaurant Tips:

Brasserie van Baerle
158 Van Baerlestraat
Tel. 020/679-1532
Open daily noon-11pm, Sun 10am-11pm, no lunch on Sat
www.brasserievanbaerle.nl

Modern brasserie (with outdoor dining in good weather) serving French cuisine. Good location in the museum district. Moderate.

Bagels and Beans
40 Van Baerlestraat
Tel. 020/675-7050
Mon -Fri 8:30am-6pm, Sat 9:30pm-6pm, Sun 10am-6pm

Excellent coffee and bagels. A great place for a quick snack while visiting the nearby museums. Inexpensive.

van Gogh Museum
7 Paulus Potterstraat
Tel. 020/570-0200
Open daily 10am-6pm (Fri until 10pm)
Admission: €10, €3 ages 13-17, under 13 free
www.vangoghmuseum.nl

More than 200 paintings, nearly 600 drawings and sketches, and hundreds of van Gogh's letters are found here. From his early 1880s paintings to the works of his later years of torment, these works demonstrate not only the development of van Gogh's art, but also of his fascinating life. You may know his famous paintings *Sunflowers* and *Self-Portrait as an Artist* (both of which you will find here), but come to see his other works. My favorite is his early work *A Pair of Shoes*. In addition to van Gogh's art, the works of such notables as Gauguin, Toulouse-Lautrec, Bernard, and Monet are also on display here, along with some of van Gogh's extensive collection of Japanese drawings.

A bookstore and cafeteria are on the ground floor. The first floor is organized by date and

SHOPPING TIP

If you're looking for up-scale shops (especially designer clothing), check out the stores on Pieter Cornelisz Hooftstraat (sometime abbreviated P.C. Hooftstraat) just a few blocks away from the Rijksmuseum.

location of where he created his works beginning in the Netherlands, then to Paris, Arles, St- Rémy-de-Provence, and Auvers-sur-Oise. The second floor has mostly drawings and a study area. The top floor contains a collection of works by van Gogh's colleagues. There's also a new wing that features temporary exhibits.

Don't miss this wonderful museum!

Houses of Seven Countries
20-30a Roemer Visscherstraat (between Leidseplein and Vondelpark)

In less than a block, you can see seven private homes built in 1894 in the architectural style of seven European countries:

#20 - German Gothic
#22 - French *château*

#24 – pink-and-white Spanish villa
#26 - Italian *palazzo*
#28 - Russian cathedral (with onion-shaped dome)
#30 - Dutch Renaissance (of course)
#30a - English cottage (now a hotel)

Who said Amsterdam doesn't have it all?

Nederlands Filmmuseum
(Netherlands Film Museum)
3 Vondelpark
Tel. 020/589-1400
Open Tue-Fri 10am-5pm, Sat 11am-5pm
Admission: Museum: €2, Cinema: €8
www.filmmuseum.nl

Film museum, library, and cinema with over 35,000 films. Private screening rooms are available to view videos. The cinema shows everything from silent films from the USA to Dutch films. Films are often based on a theme. For example, the films of Audrey Hepburn might be featured for a week followed by films directed by Martin Scorsese.

Food on the Run Tip:
Café Vertigo
3 Vondelpark
Tel. 020/612-3021

Open daily 11am-10pm
www.vertigo.nl
Popular and trendy outdoor café in the basement of the Netherlands Film Institute with an Alfred Hitchcock movie theme. Moderate.

Hollandse Manege
(Dutch Riding School)
140 Vondelstraat
Tel. 020/618-0942
Open Mon 2pm-midnight,
Tues-Fri 10am-midnight, Sat-Sun 10am-6pm
Admission: Free

This unusual sight is just down the road from the Film Museum. Although you might not think the outside looks like much, the inside will certainly be a surprise. This neo-Classical 1882 building has an open iron roof. It houses, of all things, an indoor horse riding school inspired by the Spanish Riding School in Vienna, Austria. There's a café here where you can have a drink and, if you're lucky, you'll be able to watch the instructors putting the horses through their elaborate moves.

Vondelpark
South of Leidseplein and north-west of Museumplein

This 120-acre park was named after Joost van den Vondel, a Dutch poet (there's a statue of him in the park). In the summer, it's filled with locals enjoying this large green space near the city center. Explore the paths, lakes, rose garden, bandstand, outdoor theater, and strange-looking round Blue Teahouse (Blauwe Theehuis) overlooking the lake. (In the late 1960s and early 1970s, the park was a hippie campground.) Free concerts and movies are held here in the summer.

Food on the Run Tip:
't Blauwe Theehuis
(Blue Teahouse)
5 Vondelpark
Tel. 020/662-0254
Open daily 9am-10pm
www.blauwetheehuis.nl

Take a break at this bizarre-looking 1936 teahouse in Vondelpark. Have a snack or a drink. There's a bar upstairs and an outdoor café in the summer. Moderate.

Leidseplein

Leidseplein
(Leidse Square)
*Entrances on Leidsestraat,
Marnixstraat, and Weteringschans*

This L-shaped square, formerly a gathering place for intellectuals, is now filled with tourists drinking Dutch beer at its many cafés. Of note is the interesting bridge over the Singel, an excellent example of the Amsterdam school of architecture.

ENTERTAINMENT TIP

Boom Chicago
*12 Leidseplein
Tel. 020/530-7300
Shows daily
Admission: begins at
€18
www.boomchicago.nl*

This comedy/improvisation group performs (in English) in the historic and intimate 300-seat Leidseplein Theater. Very popular with the Dutch and English-speaking tourists alike. Dine, drink, and laugh.

Restaurant Tip:
Blue Pepper
*366 Nassaukade
Tel. 020/489-7039
Open Mon-Sat 6pm-midnight*

Not your typical Indonesian restaurant. Innovative Indonesian cuisine served at this comfortable restaurant with (you guessed it) blue décor. Try the lamb. Expensive.

Holland Casino
*62 Max Euweplein (Singelgracht
at Leidseplein)
Tel. 020/521-111
Open daily 1:30pm-3am
Admission: €4
www.hollandcasino.nl*

A little bit of Las Vegas in Amsterdam. There are the familiar games of roulette, blackjack, poker, big wheel, Caribbean stud, and slot machines here, along with the less familiar table games of Sic Bo, Novo Multi Keno and Punto Banco (who comes up with these names?). There are three bars, a restaurant, and a brasserie on site. (There are three tiny Holland Casinos inside the airport.)

Restaurant Tips:
De Vrolijke Abrikoos
76 Weteringschans
Tel. 020/624-4672
Open daily 5:30pm-9:30pm

Popular and conveniently located vegetarian restaurant. Big salad selection. Moderate.

Café Americain
97 Leidsekade
(off of the Leidseplein)
Tel. 020/556-3009
Open daily noon-11pm

Part of the majestic American Hotel, this ornate and glamorous café, complete with beautiful stained-glass windows and

ENTERTAINMENT TIP

Paradiso
6-8 Weteringschans
Tel. 020/626-4521
www.paradiso.nl

Located in a former church (it still has its stained-glass windows), this unique concert venue and club is host to established and up-and-coming music acts.

Art Deco interior, makes you feel like you've stepped back in time. Moderate.

Jodenbuurt/Plantage

Holland Experience
17 Waterlooplein
Tel. 020/422-2233
Open daily 10am-6pm
Admission: €8.50, ages 4-16 €7.25
www.holland-experience.nl

Put on your 3-D glasses for this 30-minute promotional film of Holland. A good introduction for kids. You're seated on a moving platform in an aircraft seat for a Disney-style trip through Amsterdam and the Netherlands.

Waterlooplein Flea Market
Waterlooplein
Open Mon-Fri 9am-5pm, Sat 8:30am-5:30pm
Admission: Free

Lots of crap and some good bargains at this flea market on the square Waterlooplein.

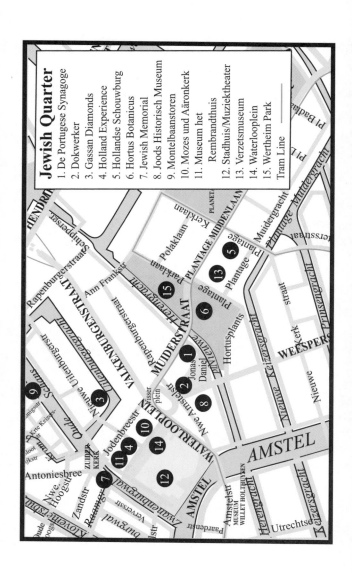

Jewish Quarter

1. De Portugese Synagoge
2. Dokwerker
3. Gassan Diamonds
4. Holland Experience
5. Hollandse Schouwburg
6. Hortus Botanicus
7. Jewish Memorial
8. Joods Historisch Museum
9. Montelbaanstoren
10. Mozes und Aäronkerk
11. Museum het Rembrandthuis
12. Stadhuis/Muziektheater
13. Verzetsmuseum
14. Waterlooplein
15. Wertheim Park

Tram Line

Montelbaanstoren
(Montelbaans Tower)
2 Oudeschans

Once part of the city's defensive wall, this tower dates back to 1516 and yes, it does slightly lean. It's now the City Water Office, the entity that regulates the water levels and cleaning of the city's canals.

Mozes en Aäronkerk
(Moses and Aaron Church)
205 Waterlooplein
Tel. 020/622-1305
Hours open vary
Admission: Free
www.mozeshuis.nl

This large, white Roman Catholic church is named after two Old Testament figures whose likenesses are found in the rear wall of the building. Its altar features the Assumption of Mary. It was built in 1641, substantially revised in the 1840s, and renovated in the 1990s. Today, it's used for exhibits and the occasional church service.

Gassan Diamonds
173 Nieuwe Uilenburgerstraat
Tel. 020/622-5333
Open daily 9am-5pm
Admission: Free
www.gassandiamonds.com

Built in 1879 shortly after diamonds were discovered in South Africa, this was home to the largest diamond-polishing and diamond-cutting factory in the world. It once employed nearly one-third of the entire Jewish population in Amsterdam. Today, you can visit the factory and its collection of jewels and, if you have the cash, purchase a diamond. The tour lasts between 60 to 90 minutes. Gassan also offers "champagne tours" for a fee, usually to groups, where at the end of the tour, everyone is given a glass of champagne and one person's glass has a real diamond in the bottom.

De Dokwerker
(The Dockworker)
Jonas Daniël Meijerplein
Open at all times
Admission: Free

Jews were forced to await deportation to concentration camps during World War II from the square Jonas Daniël Meijerplein. The bronze statue of a dockworker is a memorial to dockworkers who staged a strike in February of 1941 in protest of the deportations.

Joods Historisch Museum
(Jewish Historical Museum)
2-4 Jonas Daniël Meijerplein
Tel. 020/626-9945

*Open daily 11am-5pm, closed
Jewish holidays
Admission: €7
www.jhm.nl*

The former Jewish quarter of Amsterdam is home to this museum honoring the substantial role Jews played in Amsterdam over the last four centuries. Four former synagogues have been joined by modern structures. Jewish culture in the Netherlands and throughout the world is featured in exhibits, religious objects, paintings, photographs, and historical documents. There's also a kosher café.

Jewish Memorial
*Near Waterlooplein
at Kromboomsloot
Open at all times
Admission: Free*

This hard-to-find stone monument commemorates the 75,000 Amsterdam Jews killed during the Nazi occupation in World War II.

Stadhuis/Muziektheater
*(City Hall/Music Theater)
22 Waterlooplein/1-3 Amstel
Tel. 020/625-5455
(box office)
www.muziektheater.nl*

Built in 1986, this large modern structure on the Amstel River houses both the city hall and a concert hall (the opera and ballet perform here). It's not exactly the prettiest building in the world! Locals think it looks like dentures. You might hear it referred to as "Stopera." A combination of *stadhuis* and opera, it was coined in reaction to those who wanted to stop the destruction of medieval buildings necessary to erect this structure. There's a passageway between the City Hall and Music Theater on Waterlooplein square. Here you can see the Normal Amsterdam Level (NAP), the standard for measuring water levels in the Netherlands and all of Europe. An exhibit on sea-level management in the Netherlands (which, as you can imagine, is a big deal here with all those canals) features three glass columns that show the low tide, high tide and the incredible level the seawater reached in the 1953 floods.

Restaurant Tip:
Inez IPSC
*2 Amstel
Tel. 020/639-2899
Open Tues-Sat 7pm-10:30pm
www.inezipsc.com*

Eclectic cuisine with an excellent second-story setting on

the Muntplein. Moderate – Expensive.

Museum het Rembrandthuis
(Rembrandt House Museum)
4 Jodenbreestraat
(behind Waterlooplein)
Tel. 020/520-0400
Open Mon -Sat 10am-5pm,
Sun 11am-5pm
Admission: €8
www.rembrandthuis.nl

Rembrandt van Rijn, the famous Dutch painter, moved into this house in 1639, and lived here until his bankruptcy in 1658. In fact, papers related to his bankruptcy were used to restore its ten rooms to how they were when he resided here. The house and the modern annex contain over 250 of Rembrandt's drawings and etchings, and paintings by many of his pupils.

De Portugese Synagoge
(Portuguese Synagogue)
3 Mr. Visserplein
Tel. 020/624-5351
Open Apr-Oct Sun-Fri 10am-4pm; Nov-Mar Sun-Thurs 10am-4pm, Fri 10am-3pm; closed Jewish holidays
Admission: €7
www.esnoga.com

In 1492, Spain expelled its Jewish population. Many fled to Portugal. 100 years later, their descendents began arriving in Amsterdam. Next door to the Jewish Historical Museum, this massive structure is the largest synagogue in the world. Built in 1675, it features 12 marble columns and has survived not only time, but also the Nazi occupation in World War II. More than 1,000 candles light the giant vaulted ceiling.

De Burcht-Vakbondsmuseum
(Trade Union Museum)
9 Henri Polaklaan

ENTERTAINMENT TIP

TunFun
7 Mr. Visserplein
Tel. 020/689-4300
Open daily 10am-7pm
Admission: €7.50.
Adults are free.
Children must be accompanied by an adult
www.tunfun.nl

A huge underground indoor playground with trampolines, giant slides, children's farm, construction area and much more. If you're twelve and under, you'll love this place.

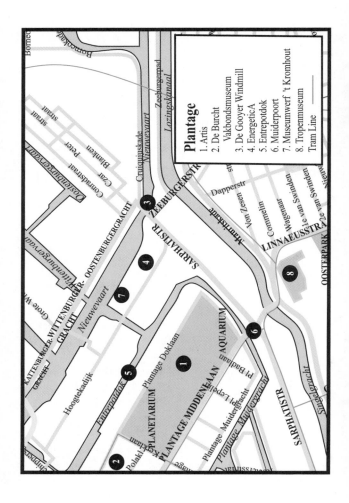

Plantage
1. Artis
2. De Burcht Vakbondsmuseum
3. De Gooyer Windmill
4. EnergeticA
5. Entrepotdok
6. Muiderpoort
7. Museumwerf 't Kromhout
8. Tropenmuseum
— Tram Line

Tel. 020/624-1166
Open Tues-Fri 11am-5pm, Sun 1pm-5pm
Admission: €3
www.deburcht-vakbondsmuseum.nl

This museum is dedicated to organized labor in the Netherlands, but the exhibit isn't nearly as impressive as the building. Built in 1900 by the same man who built the stock exchange building on Damrak, its yellow-and-white glass roof illuminates the beautiful staircase dominated by an enormous hanging lamp. The walls are blue-, yellow-, and white-glazed brick. Stained glass, carved wood paneling, and murals all give this building its nickname: "The castle."

Artis

38-40 Plantage Kerklaan
Tel. 020/523-3400
Open daily 9am-5pm (until 6pm in the summer)
Admission: €14.50, €11 ages 3-9, under 3 free. Guidebook in English available for €2.50
www.artis.nl

Amsterdam's oldest park also contains the oldest zoo in Europe. There's a planetarium, aquarium, petting zoo, elaborate playgrounds, indoor rain forest, zoological museum, geological museum, and bo-

tanical garden. Tons for kids to do!

Restaurant Tip:

De Twee Cheetahs
96 Plantage Kerklaan
Tel. 030/624-5522
Open daily 9am-5pm (until 6pm in the summer)

This restaurant (which means "the two cheetahs") overlooks the Artis Zoo's "African Savannah." Eat while you watch the zebras. Moderate.

Hortus Botanicus

(Hortus Botanical Garden)
2A Plantage Middenlaan (near Artis)
Tel. 020/625-9021
Open Mon-Fri 9am-5pm, Sat-Sun 10am-5pm, closes at 4pm Jan-Feb, closes 9pm July-Aug
Admission: €6
www.dehortus.nl

This botanical garden dates back to the 1600s. Originally a garden for medicinal herbs, it features over 8,000 plant varieties, many of which were brought here by the Dutch East Indies Company. It has a fantastic collection of tropical and subtropical plants. A peaceful and beautiful oasis in the city. Visitors can dine in the café located in the recently renovated Orangery, the former hothouse for citrus trees.

Wertheimpark
(Wertheim Park)
Between Nieuwe Herengracht
and Artis
Open daily 8am-sunset
Admission: Free

This small park along Nieuwe Herengracht is home to "Nooit Meer Auschwitz" ("Never More Auschwitz"), a memorial to those who died in the infamous concentration camp. The striking memorial resembles six pieces of shattered glass.

Hollandsche Schouwburg
(Dutch Theater)
24 Plantage Middenlaan
Tel. 020/626-9945
Open daily 11am-4pm
Admission: Free
www.hollandscheschouwburg.nl

This former theater was the deportation center for Dutch Jews under the Nazi occupation. Only the façade remains. The rest of the building is now a memorial to the over 100,000 Jews who were exterminated. The wall (to your left as you enter) displays 6,700 family names of those deported and killed. There's also an exhibit on those sent to the Westerbork concentration camp.

Verzetsmuseum
(Dutch Resistance Museum)
61 Plantage Kerklaan
Tel. 020/620-2535
Open Tues-Fri 10am-5pm, Sat-Mon noon-5pm
Admission: €5
www.verzetsmuseum.org

This interesting museum, especially to history buffs, tells the story of the Dutch Resistance (and Nazi collaborators) during World War II. Exhibits use movie clips, photos, weapons, spy gadgets, and personal testimony to tell the story of life in occupied Amsterdam between 1940 and 1945. The exhibits take you back to the 1940s by using period street scenes and house interiors. Its theme is summarized by Queen Beatrix: "If people find themselves before the inescapable choice between right and wrong, there's no certainty that they make the right decision."

Entrepotdok
Just north of Artis along Entrepotdok

These former warehouses (built in 1829) along the water just north of Artis have been rehabbed into offices, shops, apartments, and cafés. A quiet place for a walk along the canal.

Muiderpoort
Alexanderplein (along the Singelgracht)

The archway of this domed structure used to be part of the city walls. It was here that Napoleon entered the city in 1811.

De Gooyer Windmill/ Bierbrouwerij 't Ij
7 Funenkade (at Sarphatistraat) near the Kromhout Shipyard Museum
Tel. 020/622-8325
Open Wed-Sun 3pm-8pm

A microbrewery (**Bierbrouwerij 't IJ**) is housed in this old windmill (the **De Gooyer Windmill**). It's a favorite of locals, and always crowded. Enjoy one of the ten beers made here. There's a large outdoor terrace in the summer.

Museumwerf 't Kromhout
(Kromhout Shipyard Museum)
147 Hoogte Kadijk
Tel. 020/627-6777
Open Tues 10am-3pm
Admission: €5
www.machinekamer.nl/museum/engels.html

Established in 1757, this is one of the oldest shipyards in Amsterdam–and it's one of the few still repairing historic ships. This is where shipbuilding changed from wood to steel. There's also a special-interest museum featuring ships and their engines.

EnergeticA
400 Hoogte Kadijk
Tel. 020/422-1227
Open Mon-Fri 10am-4pm
Admission: €3
www.energetica.nl

Follow the history of energy production, household appliances and elevators at this museum with innovative lighting effects.

Tropenmuseum/ Kindermuseum
(Tropical and Children's Museum)
2 Linnaeusstraat at Mauritskade
Tel. 020/568-8215
Open daily 10am-5pm
Admission: €8, €4 ages 6-17, under 6 free
www.tropenmuseum.nl

The mission of this museum is an admirable one: Teach children about other cultures through re-created African, Latin-American, Caribbean and Asian villages. Most exhibits are in English. It's also a venue for many world-music concerts.

Southeast

Heineken Experience
78 Stadhouderskade
Tel. 020/523-9666
Open Tues-Sun 10am-6pm
Admission: €10
www.heinekenexperience.com

Located in the original Heineken brewery, these buildings span two centuries. This was a working brewery until 1988. You'll take a tour and drink a few beers (included in the price of admission). There's also a large gift shop for all your beer-drinking needs.

Albert Cuypmarkt
Albert Cuypstraat (between Van Woustraat and Ferdinand Bolstraat)
Open Mon-Sat 9:30am-5pm

Don't like crowds? Then don't come here. This street market is said to be Europe's busiest (especially on Saturdays). Everything from household goods to produce. Great people-watching! Lots of exotic foods and Dutch herring stands.

De Pijp
The district around the Heineken Brewery and Albert Cuypmarkt

No one is really sure how this district got its name, which means "the pipe." Some say from the brewery's tall chimneys, and others say from the long and narrow waterways once here (now filled in). It's home to many of Amsterdam's immigrants, giving the area an exotic and interesting feel. Lots of good ethnic dining.

Food on the Run Tip:
Gelateria Italiana Peppino
16 Eerste Sweelinckstraat (near
Tel. 020/676-4910
Open daily Apr-Oct 10am-11pm

Over 100 delicious flavors at this ice-cream shop located just to the east of Albert Cuypmarkt.

Sarphatipark
Two blocks south of Albert Cuypmarkt
(along Ceintuurbaan)
Open daily dawn-dusk
Admission: Free

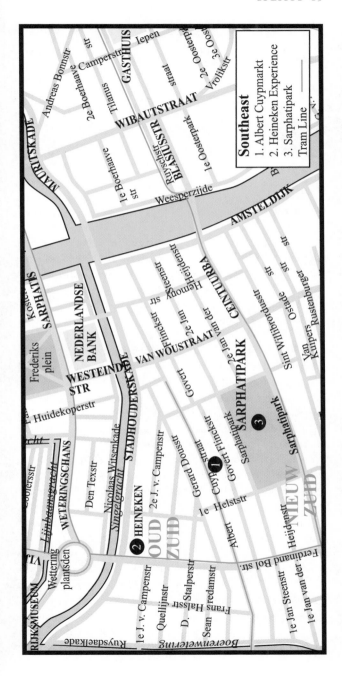

After a visit to the chaotic Albert Cuypmarkt (only two blocks away), you might want to head into this tranquil park and stroll along the paths and ponds.

Eastern Docks

NEMO
2 Oosterdok
Tel. 020/531-3233
Open Tues-Sun 10am-5pm
(open daily July-Aug)
Admission: €11, €7 students
www.e-NEMO.nl

The building that houses this science and technology museum is in the shape of a huge green ship, which is appropriate for its harborside location. It's perfect for children, and its interactive and entertaining exhibits are in both Dutch and English. The rooftop café offers great views of the city. (You reach this museum by walking on several footbridges to the east of Centraal Station).

Restaurant Tip:
Sea Palace
8 Oosterdokskade
Tel. 020/626-4777
Open daily noon-11pm
www.seapalace.nl

Claiming to be the first float-ing restaurant in Europe, the Sea Palace opened in 1984. It's huge. There are three floors that can accommodate 700 diners (mostly tourists). Eat Chinese dishes such as Peking duck and dim sum and enjoy the view. Moderate – Expensive.

Scheepvaartmuseum
(Maritime Museum)
1 Kattenburgerplein at Prins Hendrikkade
Tel. 020/523-2222
Open Tues-Sun 10am-5pm
(also open Mon mid-June-mid-Sept)
Admission: €8, €4 ages 6-16, under 6 free
www.scheepvaartmuseum.nl

The Dutch have relied upon the sea for centuries. This museum is housed in the National Naval Depot, a 300-year-old former arsenal of the Dutch Navy. Historic ships are docked outside, including *The Amsterdam* with its three tall masts. Actors reenact life

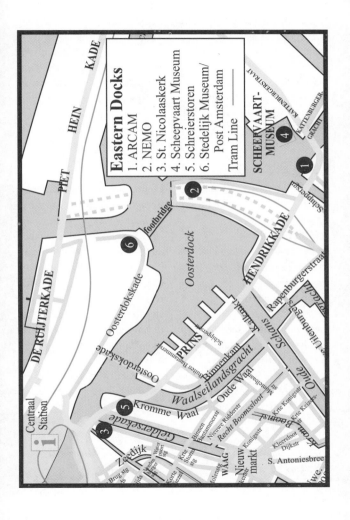

Eastern Docks

1. ARCAM
2. NEMO
3. St. Nicolaaskerk
4. Scheepvaart Museum
5. Schreierstoren
6. Stedelijk Museum/
   Post Amsterdam

Tram Line ————

on board the ship. There are boats inside, too, including the ornate royal barge. There are more than 25 rooms featuring model ships, paintings, old sailing vessels, racing boats, luxury passenger ships, and giant container ships (it's a huge museum). A must for boat lovers. Note that it's one of the few museums in Amsterdam without English translations.

Restaurant Tip:

Vermeer
59-72 Prins Hendrikkade
(in the NH Barbizon Palace Hotel)
Tel. 020/556-4885
Open Mon-Fri noon-2:30pm for lunch, Mon-Sat 6pm-10pm for dinner
www.restaurantvermeer.nl

Elegant dining under chandeliers in this restaurant in the NH Barbizon Palace Hotel. Attentive waiters serve innovative French cuisine on Delft plates. Very Expensive.

St. Nicolaaskerk
(St. Nicholas Church)
76 Prins Hendrikkade
Open daily (hours vary)
Admission: Free

St. Nicholas is the patron saint of seafarers. This huge church dates back to 1887, and was built after the anti-Catholic laws were repealed in 1821. It's one of the first buildings visitors see as they leave Centraal Station. There are masses held here in Dutch, Spanish and English. Lots of incense. A beautiful choral evensong is sung every Saturday at 5 p.m. from September to June.

Schreierstoren
(Weeping Tower)
94-95 Prins Hendrikkade

Henry Hudson set sail from here to find a shorter route to the East Indies. What he found instead was the Hudson River and New Amsterdam (now New York City). This tower was once part of a defensive stone wall built around the city in the late 1400s. It's said to have gotten its name from the weeping women who came here to send their men to far-off destinations. It now houses a café.

Amsterdam Center for Architecture (ARCAM)
600 Prins Hendrikkade
Tel. 020/620-4878
Open Tues-Sat 1pm-5pm
Admission: Free
www.arcam.nl

ARCAM features changing exhibits on architecture, landscape architecture, and urban development. It's located in a new space-age building near the Maritime Museum.

Post Amsterdam
5 Oosterdokskade (near Centraal Station)
Tel. 020/421-1033
Open Mon-Sat 11am-5pm, Sun noon-5pm
Admission: Free
www.postamsterdam.nl

Post Amsterdam (formerly Pakhuis Amsterdam) is located in an unattractive building just east of Centraal Station. You reach it by walking over several footbridges over the water. A must for those interested in interior design. It's in the same building as the temporary home of the **Stedelijk Museum of Mod-**ern Art. Take the service elevator to the 11th floor (where there is a café, restaurant and club) and walk down to the 10th and 9th floors. An added bonus is the great views of all of Amsterdam.

ENTERTAINMENT TIP

Bimhuis
3 Piet Heinkade
Tel. 020/788-2150
Open for events
Admission: Depends on the event
www.bimhuis.nl

Interested in hearing some jazz? Bimhuis features over 200 jazz and improv music concerts each year. Now in its new modern digs.

Haarlemmerbuurt/Western Islands

Haarlemmerbuurt
Directly north of the Jordaan

This mostly residential neighborhood is north of the Jordaan neighborhood. On Haarlemmerstraat is the **Westindisch Huis**, the former headquarters of the Dutch West Indies Company, the company established to colonize America. It was here that the sale of Manhattan and the decision to transfer West Africans to the Caribbean as slaves took place. In the courtyard off of Herenmarkt (at number 99) is the statue of

THE DUTCH EXPLORERS

In the early 1600s, the Dutch began to establish overseas colonies. The Dutch East Indies Company was founded in 1602 and the Dutch West Indies Company in 1621. A spice trade grew out of Indonesia, and trade with North America and South America, especially Brazil, brought treasures back home.

Peter Stuyvesant, who was the director of all Dutch possessions in North America and the Caribbean. In 1647 he arrived in New Amsterdam (later New York City), and in 1664 was forced to surrender it to the British. He spent the rest of his life on his farm, "the Bouwerie," from which New York City's "Bowery" takes its name.

Restaurant Tip:
Lof
62 Haarlemmerstraat
Tel. 020/620-2997
Open Tues-Sat 6pm-11pm
No credit cards

There's no menu at this informal and hip restaurant. The waiters tell you what is avail-able each day. Interesting international cuisine. Moderate.

Haarlemmerpoort
50 Haarlemmerplein

A neo-Classical-style, ornate gatehouse built in 1840. It's sometimes referred to as Willemspoort as it was built in honor of King William II. It's at the northern end of the Jordaan neighborhood to the east of the Westerpark park.

Westergasfabriek
(West Gas Factory)
8-10 Haarlemmerweg
Tel. 020/586-0710
Open for events
www.westergasfabriek.com

This former gas plant has been renovated and transformed into a venue for concerts and theater. There's a lively bar and restaurant, and a park where there once was an industrial complex. Truly an interesting redevelopment of a former industrial site.

Westelijke Eilanden
(Western Islands)
Northwest of Centraal Station

The three manmade islands that make up the Western Islands are Realeneiland, Prinseneiland, and Bickerseiland. Made in the 17th century, they are now an interesting mix of old warehouses and modern development. The smallest island, Prinseneiland, is filled with old warehouses and boatyards. The largest island, Bickerseiland, has warehouses and modern development. Realeneiland (reached by an old wooden drawbridge) is home to the lovely Zandhoek, an attractive row of houses built in the 1600s, on the eastern shore of the island. (The islands are reached by buses 18 or 22).

Restaurant Tip:
De Gouden Reael
14 Zandhoek
Tel. 020/623-3883
Open daily 11am-11pm
www.goudenreael.nl

Stop at this attractive café and restaurant while visiting the Western Islands. If the weather is nice, have a seat on the terrace with views of the water and old wooden bridge. You can dine here on French cuisine in a 17th-century canal house. Moderate.

Off the Beaten Path

WTC Amsterdam
(Amsterdam World Trade Center)
1 Strawinskylaan (on Zuidplein and along highway A-10)
Tel. 020/575-9111
Metro to WTC/Zuid station
www.wtcamsterdam.com

If you're in Amsterdam on business, you may find yourself at the World Trade Center, home to hundreds of international companies. Opened in 1985 (and recently renovated), the building is known as the "Blue Angel" and has won several architectural design awards.

Zuidas
Metro to WTC/Zuid station
www.zuidas.nl

This new section of Amsterdam has been developed around the World Trade Center. Most pass this "south axle" of the city on their way into town from Schiphol Airport. Its goal is to be the Amsterdam of the future. Check out the silver-and-glass shoe-shaped **ING House**, the headquarters of the

International Netherlands Group (ING) Bank at 500 Amstelveenseweg. Very weird. Only come to this commercial center if you're a big fan of modern architecture.

Museum Vrolik

15 Meibergdreef (in the Department of Medicine of the Amsterdam Medical Center)
Tel. 020/566-4927
Open Mon-Fri 9:30am-5pm
Admission: Free
From Centraal Station, take the Metro in the direction of Gein and get out at the Holendrecht station

In the southeastern suburbs of Amsterdam on the campus of the Amsterdam Medical Center is one of the most bizarre "museums" in the world. It's named after Willem and Gerardus Vrolik, a father and son, who collected animal and human specimens. Human bones ravaged by disease, 150 deformed fetuses in formaldehyde ... do I need to go on? This is extreme, even by Amsterdam standards!

Beatrixpark

South of Vondelpark and next to the RAI Convention and Exhibition Center
Open daily dawn-dusk
Admission: Free

From Centraal Station, take Metro 51 to RAI station

This lovely park, named after the queen, is a great place to get away from it all. A pond filled with swans, play areas for children, and a Victorian walled garden all make this a great place to relax. Less crowded than Vondelpark.

RAI

22 Europaplein
Tel. 020/549-1212
www.rai.nl
From Centraal Station, take Metro 51 to RAI station

If you're visiting Amsterdam to attend a trade convention, it's likely that you'll see a lot of the RAI, Amsterdam's exhibition and convention center.

Amstelpark

South of Vondelpark and bordered on the west
by Europaboulevard
Open daily dawn-dusk
Admission: Free
From Centraal Station, take Metro 51 to RAI station

Like Beatrixpark, this park is less crowded than Vondelpark. Children will love the petting zoo and miniature train while adults can take it easy wandering around the rose garden.

The Amstelpark is home to one of the few remaining windmills, **De Rieker Windmill**. This one dates back to 1636, and is located at the southern tip of the park. A great photo opportunity, but it's now someone's home, so you can't go inside.

AMSTERDAM PARKS

Amsterdam has 28 parks. In addition to those listed above, there are also these great places to relax and have a picnic:

Martin Luther Kingpark: Next to the Amstel River off President Kennedylaan northeast of Amstel Park (in the southern part of the city).

Oosterpark: In the eastern part of the city (where the Tropenmuseum is located) along Oosterparkstraat.

Rembrandtpark: In the western part of the city along Jan Evertsenstraat.

Westerpark: In the northwestern part of the city along Haarlemmerweg.

Flevopark: In the eastern part of the city along Flevoweg (further east than Oosterpark).

Elektrische
Museum Tramlijn
(Tram Museum)
264 Amstelveenseweg
Tel. 020/673-7538
Open Sun and holidays from Easter through October
Admission: €5
www.museumtram.nl
(in Dutch)

Trams dating from 1910 from the Netherlands and other European countries take you on 20-minute trips from Haarlemmermeerstation past such sites as the Olympic Stadium. You reach the museum by (surprise!) taking tram 16 to Haarlemmermeerstation.

Amsterdamse Bos
(Amsterdam Woods)
In the suburb of Amstelveen (a few miles south of the city with the main entrance on Amstelveenseweg)
Open daily 10am-5pm
Admission: Free

With over 2,200 acres, this is the largest of Amsterdam's parks. Features include a pond (**Grote Vijver**); a rowing stadium; a petting zoo for children; a large goat farm; rowing boat, kayak and bike rentals; over 30 miles of bicycle paths; nearly 90 miles of walking and running paths; an open-air theater (**Openluchttheater**) for summer concerts; a Cherry-Blossom Park (**Kersenbloesempark**) with 400 cherry trees; and the free natural history museum (**Bosmuseum**). Take bus 170, 171, or 172 from Centraal Station.

Cobra Museum
voor Moderne Kunst
(Cobra Museum)
1 Sandbergplein (In the suburb of Amstelveen (a few miles south of the city)
Tel. 020/547-5050
Open Tues -Sun 11am-5pm
Admission: €7, €3 under 17
www.cobra-museum.nl
From Centraal Station, take tram 5 to Amstelveen Binnenhof stop

This museum is filled with modern paintings, sculpture, and ceramics. The founders of the Cobra movement created its name by combining the names of their home cities: Copenhagen, Brussels and Amsterdam. This modern-art movement wanted art to be inclusive and spontaneous, and was inspired by primitive art and even the art of the mentally ill. The museum has the world's only Karel Appel fountain (he's one of the founders, and a Dutch Abstract Expressionist painter). Tours and brochures in English.

Olympisch Stadion
(Olympic Stadium)
2 Olympisch Stadion (along route A10 in the southwestern part of town)
Tel. 020/671-1115
www.olympisch-stadion.net
From Centraal Station, take tram 16 or 24 to Stadionplein stop

Amsterdam was the host of the 1928 Olympics. The renovated stadium (saved from demolition) is located in the southwest section of town and still hosts some sporting events. Although it's usually closed, you can get a view of the stadium at the very trendy café/bar/restaurant **Café Vak Zuid** (closed Saturday and Sunday mornings).

Excursions Outside Amsterdam

Holland is small enough that, given its great public transportation system, you can get to nearly any part of the country in less than two hours.

NATIONAAL LUCHTVAART THEMAPARK AND AVIODROME
(National Aviation Museum and Themepark)
50 Pelikaanweg in Lelystad
Tel. 320289840
Open daily 9am-5pm
Admission: €14, €12 ages 4-12
www.aviodrome.nl
From Schiphol Airport take the train from platform 2 to Lelystad. From Lelystad station, take Connexxion bus 148 to the Vliegveld/Eendeweg stop. It's a few minutes walk to the Lelystad Airport. By car from the airport, go in the direction of Utrecht. Then take A1 in the direction of Amersfoort/Almere until route A6. Follow this route in the direction of Lelystad. Take the Lelystad exit (N302), go left at the traffic signs (direction Harderwijk) and follow the signs to Lelystad Airport/Aviodrome

This museum and theme park celebrates 100 years of aviation. It's located in the Aviodrome, at Lelystad airport (45 minutes from Amsterdam). A "time machine" takes you back to 1896, showing key events in aviation history. You can board the 1930s "Pelikaan," a pre-war KLM airplane, and experience what air travel was like then. A theater simulates a ride in a hot-air balloon flying over the sites of the Netherlands. Lots of interactive exhibits, including a jet-fighter flight simulator. A must for those interested in aviation.

EDAM
14 miles (22 km) northeast of Amsterdam.
No train service. Buses (110, 112, 114 and 116) depart hourly from Centraal Station. By car, take route A1 to exit S116 in the direction of Volendam
www.vvv-edam.nl

This small village of 7,000 people is known for its red wax-covered cheese (the local

version is covered in yellow wax). Most come here for the colorful weekly **cheese market** on Wednesday mornings during July and August where locals, dressed in traditional costumes, carry the cheese to the **Kaaswaag** (Weigh House). Don't just come here to see and taste cheese. Edam is a lovely town with beautiful buildings (such as the 15th-century **St. Nicolaas church**), tranquil canals, picturesque drawbridges, and lots of cafés.

Stadhuis
(Town Hall)
1 Damplein (town center)
Tel. 029/931-5125 (tourist information)
Open Apr-Oct Tues-Sat 10am-4:30pm, Sun 1:30pm-4:30pm
Admission: Free

Built in the 18th century, the Town Hall has a beautifully painted civic room known as the "wedding room."

Carillon
Damplein (town center)

This slender late-Gothic tower on the main square dates back to the 15th century. Its bells were made in 1566.

Edams Museum
8 Damplein (town center)
Tel. 029/937-2644
Open Tues-Sat 10am-4:30pm, Sun 1:30pm-4:30pm
Admission: €3

Edam was once a thriving port. This museum, in the oldest brick house in town, takes you back to life in the 1600s. Check out the three portraits of townsfolk (especially the guy with the long red beard). In addition to furnishings and portraits, you can visit the cellar that was built to float.

HAARLEM
12 miles (19 km) west of Amsterdam (route A5 in the direction of Haarlem)
Many trains daily from Centraal Station. 20-minute trip (about €12 round-trip)

Haarlem is an easy day-trip from Amsterdam. It has a lovely market square, compact historic center, 16th- and 17th-century buildings, and canals. It's a smaller and more sedate version of Amsterdam. Most major sights are within easy walking distance of each other.

Grote Markt
(Market Square)
Center of town

Loaded with cafés, this car-free square in the center of town is the home of an impressive **Stadhuis** (Town Hall), parts of which date back to the mid-1300s. There's a huge market on Saturdays and a clothing market on Mondays.

Grote Kerk/Sint Bavokerk

(Great Church/St. Bavo Church)
Grote Markt (enter at 23 Oude Groenmarkt)
Tel. 023/553-2040
Open Mon-Sat 10am-4pm, Sun for services
Admission: €2
www.bavo.nl

Dominating Market Square is the huge church Sint Bavokerk (also known as the Grote Kerk). In its floor are over 1,350 graves, including that of painter Frans Hals (see Frans Hals Museum below). Those black marks on the central pillar are of the town's tallest and shortest residents. The shortest resident is said to have been a dwarf who died in a game he allegedly invented: Dwarf-tossing! Look up at the impressive vaulted cedar ceiling. The real star here is the ornate church organ built in 1738, featuring over 5,000 pipes that was played by both Mozart and Handel. Organ concerts are frequently held here.

De Hallen

16 Grote Markt
Tel. 023/511-5775
Open Tues-Sat 11am-5pm, Sun noon-5pm
Admission: €4
www.dehallen.com

Two lovely buildings in the center of town house this modern-art museum with an impressive collection of contemporary photography. The Verweyhal building was built in 1879 for a gentlemen's society in the neo-Classical style, and later renovated in Art Deco style. In 1992 it was transformed into an exhibition hall for the Frans Hals Museum (see below). The Vleeshal building is an example of Dutch Renaissance architecture. Built in 1602, the decorations on the outside represent its original use as a meat market.

Restaurant Tip:

Jacobus Pieck
18 Warmoesstraat (from Grote Markt to Lepelaarstraat, cross Spekstraat to Warmoesstraat)
Tel. 023/532-6144
Open Mon-Sat 11am-4pm for lunch, Tues-Sat 5:30pm-10pm for dinner

No-frills dining on local specialties served indoors and outdoors on the terrace. Good place for a salad. Inexpensive - Moderate.

Frans Hals Museum
62 Groot Heiligland
Tel. 023/511-5775
Open Tues-Sat 11am-5pm,
Sun noon-5pm
Admission: €7
www.franshalsmuseum.nl

This former old-age home and orphanage houses a museum with an impressive collection of 16th- and 17th-century paintings (especially large group portraits) along with a collection of Delftware, craft objects, and period furnishings. The museum is named after Frans Hals, the 17th-century painter known for his portraits. The museum is arranged around a lovely courtyard restored to how it looked in the 17th century.

Teylers Museum
16 Spaarne
Tel. 023/531-9010
Open Tues-Sat 11am-5pm,
Sun noon-5pm
Admission: €6
www.teylersmuseum.nl (in Dutch)

This is the Netherlands's oldest museum. It's known for its huge collection of over 10,000 drawings by such notables as Michelangelo, Raphael, and Rembrandt. Exhibits feature ancient scientific instruments, early electronics, fossils, and minerals. (It has a bizarre-looking electrostatic generator dating back to 1784.)

Corrie ten Boom House
19 Barteljorisstraat
Tel. 023/531-0823
Open Apr-Oct Tues-Sat 10am-3:30pm, Nov-Mar 11am-2:30pm
Admission: Donation

Corrie Ten Boom wrote a book (later turned into a movie) called *The Hiding Place*, which told the story of her family's efforts to hide Jews from the Nazis during the occupation. Jews were hidden by the family in a small room on the top floor. The family was arrested on suspicion of assisting "the enemy" and while Corrie survived the concentration camp, her father and sister did not. Interestingly, the Jews who were hiding in the secret room were able to escape. There are hour-long tours (in English), but be warned, they can be quite preachy.

Red-Light District
Two blocks from Market Square off of Lange Begijnestraat

Haarlem has a smaller, and

somewhat less seedy, version of Amsterdam's Red-Light District. To give you that extra taste of Amsterdam, there are also a few coffeeshops in the area.

DELFT
40 miles (65 km) south of Amsterdam (Route A4 in the direction of Rotterdam. Delft exit or route A13 to Delft South exit)
Many trains daily from Centraal Station. One-hour trip (about €20 round trip)

Delft dates back to 1075. A huge explosion at the national arsenal (oops!) leveled the town in the mid-1600s. The town was rebuilt, and little has changed since then. It's one of the best-preserved towns in the Netherlands, and is best known for Delftware, handpainted blue-and-white china. But don't come to Delft just to look at a bunch of dishes. Beautiful tree-lined canals, narrow cobblestone streets, charming pedestrian bridges, graceful mansions, antiques shops (selling lots of Delftware) and outdoor cafés all make this town a wonderful day-trip. If you have the time, the beauty of Delft is best experienced if you stay overnight, when all the day-trippers leave.

De Porceleyne Fles
196 Rotterdamseweg
Tel. 015/251-2030
Open daily 9am-5pm, closed Sun Nov-Mar
Admission: €5
www.royaldelft.com

You can see Delftware, the famous handpainted blue-and-white china, made at this factory.

Lambert van Meerten
199 Oude Delft
Phone 015/260-2358
Open Tues-Sat 10am-5pm, Sun 11am-5pm

PARIS MADE EASY

How about dinner in Paris? It's possible. You can be in Paris in a mere four hours. The Thalys high-speed train takes you from Centraal Station to Gare du Nord in Paris for around €100 roundtrip allowing you to visit Amsterdam and Paris in the same day. Reservations can be made at *www.thalys.com* (a somewhat confusing website) or through your travel agent. For more information on visiting Paris, pick up Open Road's *Paris Made Easy.*

Admission: €5
www.gemeentemusea-delft.nl

Located in a lovely 19th-century mansion, this is where you come to see antique Delftware.

Nieuwe Kerk
(New Church)
Markt (Market Square)
Tel. 015/212-3025
Open Apr-Oct Mon-Sat 9am-6pm, Nov-Mar Mon-Sat 11am-4pm, Sun services at 10am
Admission: €3 (includes entry to the Oude Kerk)
www.nieuwekerk-delft.nl

This 14th-century Gothic church is the burial place for the royal family. You can't miss the tomb of William of Orange, it's the one with the golden statue of the prince. Check out the 17th-century pulpit with cherubs that look like they're sliding down the rope.

Restaurant Tip:
Café Vlaanderen
16 Beestenmarkt
Tel. 015/213-3311
Open daily at noon (weekends at 11am)
www.vlaanderen.nl

The lovely Beestenmarkt (near Market Square) is home to this café and restaurant serving international fare. You can dine in the restaurant, on the square or in the garden. Moderate - Expensive.

Oude Kerk
(Old Church)
Heilige Geestkerkhof
Tel. 015/212-3015
Open Apr-Oct Mon-Sat 9am-6pm, Nov-Mar Mon-Sat 11am-4pm, Sun services at 10am
Admission: €3 (includes entry to the Nieuwe Kerk)
www.oudekerk-delft.nl

No, you didn't have too much wine with lunch. The church's tower is leaning. Inside is the elaborately carved wooden pulpit and the graves of famous locals, including the 17th-century Dutch painter Jan Vermeer.

Prinsenhof
1 Sint Agathaplein
Tel. 015/260-2358
Open Tues-Sat 10am-5pm, Sun 1pm-5pm
Admission: €5
www.gemeentemusea-delft.nl

A museum of the history of the House of Orange is located in this 15th-century former convent and royal residence. William of Orange was assassinated here (you can still see the bullet holes in the staircase). Lots of tapestries, royal portraits, and (you guessed it) Delftware.

Restaurant Tip:
Stadsherberg de Mol
104 Molslaan
Tel. 015/212-1343
Open Tues-Sun 6pm-9:30pm
www.stadsherbergdemol.nl

Be a tourist! This medieval inn, located in a historic former home, serves fixed-priced meals (around €20). Servers are dressed in traditional costumes. But there's a catch: You have to eat as you would have in the Middle Ages (no utensils). There's also medieval music and dancing. It's not for everyone, but groups really like it.

AALSMEER
9 miles (16 km) southwest of Amsterdam (From route A10, take route A4 in the direction of The Hague. Take exit 3 in the direction of Aalsmeer[route N201]). Near the airport. Bus number 172 from Centraal Station (one-hour trip)

Verenigde Bloemenveilingen
(Flower Auction)
Tel. 0297/392-185 or 398-050
Open Mon-Fri 7:30am-11:00pm

Admission: €5
www.bloemenveiling-aalsmeer.nl

The Netherlands is the world's largest exporter of cut flowers–and half of them come through this auction, the largest of its kind in the world. You can view the fields of flowers in what is said to be the world's largest commercial building. The auction building covers 160 acres. Every day nearly 19 million flowers and plants are auctioned, and there's a gallery to watch the proceedings. Although it's not for everyone, the sight of all those cut flowers and potted plants is amazing and an incredible photo opportunity. Best time to visit is before 9:00 a.m. (Monday is the busiest day and it's slowest on Thursdays.)

BOLLENSTREEK
(Bulb District)
From Haarlem south to Leiden. You can drive south from Amsterdam on route A4 (in the direction of Leiden), past the airport to the junction Nieuw Vennep, then northeast on route N207 toward Lisse

If you're in Amsterdam during the spring (especially April and May) and interested in seeing incredible fields of flowers such as tulips, daffodils, and ama-ryllis, the Bulb District is a spectacular sight. The route is along a 25-mile, Haarlem-to-Leiden drive. The route is marked by blue-and-white signs that say "Bollenstreek."

BRINGING TULIPS HOME

If you want to bring tulips home, make sure that the package has a sticker on it that says "with health certificate for US and Canada." You'll need the health certificate (usually pasted on the back of the package) and make sure that the certificate has not expired. Most bulbs sold at the airport come with the certificate.

2. WALKS

Major Sights Walk

Highlights: Dam Square, Beguine Court, and Flower Market. See Major Sights map on the next page. Approximate length of walk: one mile.

Our walk begins at the Stationsplein, the bustling square in front of Centraal Station. With Centraal Station to your back, cross the Open Haven Front (that's the body of water right in front of the Stationsplein). The street in front of you is Damrak.

The first street that most travelers to Amsterdam explore is **Damrak**, the main street connecting Centraal Station and Dam Square. It's filled with fast-food outlets, and souvenir shops selling everything from wooden shoes to Dutch chocolate. It's probably Amsterdam's least attractive street.

Head down Damrak. You'll pass the Sex Museum on your right (you can visit that on the "Naughty Walk") and the huge Beurs van Berlage (the former stock exchange) on your left. It's now used as a convention center and is home to the Netherlands Philharmonic Orchestra. Soon you'll reach a large square. You can't miss it.

DETOUR

Need a drink before you visit the major sights on this walk? Take a right off of Damrak onto Zoutsteeg. This little street is just before the De Bijenkorf, Amsterdam's best-known department store (on the left side of Damrak). At number 7 Zoutsteeg is Helen van Troye, the self-proclaimed smallest pub in Amsterdam. Have a drink at this friendly bar.

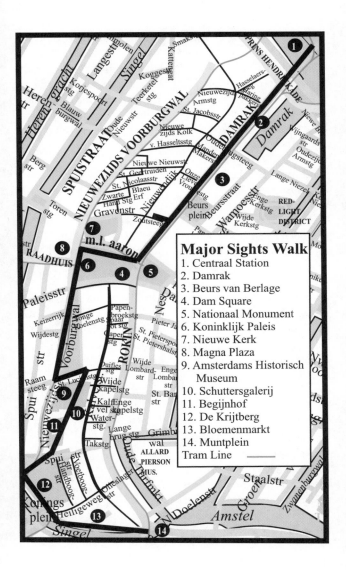

Major Sights Walk
1. Centraal Station
2. Damrak
3. Beurs van Berlage
4. Dam Square
5. Nationaal Monument
6. Koninklijk Paleis
7. Nieuwe Kerk
8. Magna Plaza
9. Amsterdams Historisch Museum
10. Schuttersgalerij
11. Begijnhof
12. De Krijtberg
13. Bloemenmarkt
14. Muntplein
Tram Line ———

You're now at Dam Square. The 70-foot white obelisk here is the **National Monument** (Nationaal Monument). It was built in 1956 as a war memorial dedicated to those who endured World War II and the Nazi occupation. The urns at the back of the monument contain earth from each Dutch province and its former colonies: Indonesia, The Netherlands Antilles in the Caribbean, and Suriname in South America.

The massive **Royal Palace** (Koninklijk Paleis) was built in the mid-1600s (closed Mondays except in July and August). Originally it served as City Hall, became a royal residence under the rule of Napoleon, and a royal palace of the House of Orange. The royal family doesn't live here anymore.

Head for the public entrance of the Royal Palace.

The marble-floored **Citizens Chamber** (Burgerzaal) runs the length of the second floor of the palace. You'll find mighty Atlas holding a globe and maps in the floor portraying Amsterdam as the center of the world.

As you face the Royal Palace, head to your right to the large church.

The **New Church** (Nieuwe Kerk) dates back to the early 1400s. Check out its stark interior as this former Catholic church lost most of its decorations and statues during the Iconoclasm of 1566 (when the Protestants destroyed the icons, statues and other decorations of Catholic churches). It now houses changing exhibits.

Now we are heading for a street with the long name of Nieuwezijds Voorburgwal (behind the Royal Palace and Dam Square). The opulent building at 182 used to be a post office. Now it's all about shopping.

The **Magna Plaza** was built in 1899 and now it houses over 40 stores on five stories. Go inside if you're in the mood to shop. Closed Sunday mornings.

Continue down Nieuwezijds Voorburgwal (to your right with the Magna Plaza to your back). Turn left onto Sint Luciënsteeg. At number 27 is one of three entrances to one of the best museums in Amsterdam, the Amsterdams Historisch Museum. Enter the courtyard. To your right is the museum entrance.

Before you enter the museum,

notice the 47 wall plaques preserved from buildings throughout the city that were either demolished or renovated.

The **Amsterdam Historical Museum** (Amsterdams Historisch Museum), once a 17th-century orphanage, chronicles the history of Amsterdam from fishing village to modern metropolis. You'll find paintings (including Rembrandt's partly damaged and ghastly *Anatomy Lecture of Dr Jan Deijman*), maps, wearing apparel, jewelry, prints, porcelain, sculpture and archeological finds.

If you don't want to visit the museum (or if you have finished your visit to the museum), head to your left. In between the courtyard of the Amsterdam Historical Museum and the Begijnhof is our next sight.

The **Civic Guards Gallery** (Schuttersgalerij) is a glass-covered passageway filled with a group of huge early 1600s portraits of the city's civic guards who were initially responsible for the safety of the city, but later became fraternal groups.

At the end of the gallery, exit out onto Gedempte Begijnensloot. Walk a short while down this narrow alley until you see the entrance to the courtyard on your right side. Enter the courtyard.

The Beguine Court (Begijnhof) is open daily until sunset. The courtyard of this 14th-century *hofje* (almshouse) is a peaceful getaway from the bustling city. Founded in 1346 by members of a lay Catholic sisterhood (the Beguines), it's still the home of elderly poor women. There's a statue of a Beguine, dressed in traditional habit, in the center. You can see the **English Reformed Church** (Engelse Kerk) dating back to the late 1300s, and the **Mother Superior's House** (number 26). The **Begijnhof Chapel** opposite the English Reformed Church houses a clandestine church (like Our Dear Lord of the Attic above).

Cornelia Arents was the mother superior of the Beguines and died in 1654. She was buried in the English Reformed Church against her wishes (she was a Roman Catholic and did not wish to be buried in a Protestant church). Arents is said to have announced that she would rather be buried in the gutter. According to legend, the morning after her burial, her coffin was found in the gutter next to the lawn outside the church. That's why you'll see a grave in the gutter. A wall plaque next to the lawn outside the church reads "Beguine Cornelia Arents was laid to rest in this gutter at her own request. May 2, 1654."

Look for number 34.

At number 34 in this courtyard is the **City's Oldest House** (Het Houten Huis). It dates back to about 1475.

After passing the oldest house, head through the arched doorway. Follow the stairs that lead to the square Spui.

The small **Spui** square is filled with bookshops, bars and cafés. **Café Hoppe**, a brown café (brown from all of the cigarette smoke that has darkened its walls) has been in business for over 300 years. The statue **Little Darling** (Het Lieverdje) here is of an urchin (the one with hands on hips). It's said to be a symbol of Amsterdam: Always full of life and a little mischievous. There's a book market here on Fridays and an art market on Sundays. A great place to stop at a café.

Take a right and walk straight to the pedestrian-only street Heisteeg. Continue over the bridge Heiburg and then take a left at Singel. Our next sight is at number 446.

You can't miss the two steeples of this 1880s neo-Gothic church. The name **De Krijtberg** means "chalk church" since the church was built on the site of a home owned by a chalk merchant. Its real name is **St. Francis Xavier Church** (Franciscus Xaveriuskerk). Head inside to take a look at the statue of St. Francis Xavier to the left of the altar, the detailed wood carving of the Immaculate Conception near the pulpit, and the statue of St. Ignatius, the founder of the Jesuits, to the right of the altar.

Continue down the Singel. Our next sight is between Koningsplein and Muntplein.

Stalls selling cut flowers and bulbs are sold from "floating" anchored barges on the Singel Canal. The Flower Market (Bloemenmarkt), closed Sunday, is incredibly fragrant, and a great photo opportunity. If you buy bulbs to take back home, make sure they have a sticker on them saying that they are approved by Customs to bring into the country.

At the end of the Flower Market is Muntplein.

The **Mint Tower** (Munttoren) on the square **Muntplein** gets its name from the time when it was used as a mint during the French occupation of the city in the 1600s. Its bells ring every 15 minutes. You can end your walk at one of the cafés here.

Naughty Walk

Highlights: Sex Museum, Red-Light District, and Hash Marijuana Hemp Museum. See Naughty Walk map on the next page. Approximate length of walk: one mile.

Our walk begins at the Stationsplein, the bustling square in front of Centraal Station. With Centraal Station to your back, cross the Open Haven Front (that's the body of water right in front of the Stationsplein). The street in front of you is Damrak. Walk down Damrak until you reach number 18 (on your right).

Eroticism from Greco-Roman times to today is featured at the Sex Museum. Everything from erotic art to ancient phallic symbols (read: dildos) to vintage porn films.

Continue down Damrak until you reach Oude Brugsteeg. It's the first street to your left; head straight toward Warmoesstraat. It's the street where the large neon "Sex Shop" sign is. Take a right onto Warmoesstraat.

On Warmoesstraat you'll pass sex shops, porn stores, cafés selling marijuana (more about that later), gay leather bars, and pubs.

Walk down Warmoesstraat and take a left at Enge Kerksteeg. Walk down this street past the Prostitution Information Center (seriously!). You'll now see our next sight.

The **Old Church** (Oude Kerk) is indeed Amsterdam's oldest. Parts of it date back to the 13th century. Today this Gothic basilica is almost totally surrounded by the Red-Light District. It has a world-famous organ dating back to 1724 and a restored carillon.

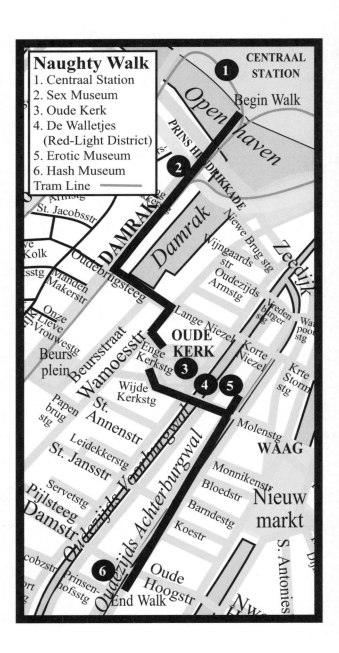

Naughty Walk
1. Centraal Station
2. Sex Museum
3. Oude Kerk
4. De Walletjes
   (Red-Light District)
5. Erotic Museum
6. Hash Museum
Tram Line

The organ stands on marble pillars that were cleaned and restored in the late 1970s. It's said that you can see the restorer's face in the marble (to the left above floor level). Its beautiful stained-glass windows (depicting the death of the Virgin Mary), decorated pillars, 15th-century carved choir stalls and painted ceiling make this landmark a must for all visitors. There's a great view of the surrounding Red-Light District if you want to climb up the 16th-century bell tower.

DETOUR

An unknown artist has left bronze and iron artwork throughout the city over the past fifteen years. See if you can find the bronze woman's bust covered by a hand embedded in the bricks facing Oudekerksplein.

All around the Old Church is the Red-Light District.

The Red-Light District (De Walletjes) puts a new spin on window-shopping. The oldest profession, legal here since 1984, has its "headquarters" along the narrow streets of the Red-Light District, where women wait in windows for their next customer. The storefront rooms have curtains which are closed when "business" is being conducted. You'll see lots of foreign businessmen and tourists milling around (many very drunk). Be careful at night, as the area is a prime pickpocket spot. By the way, don't even think about taking photos. Your camera will likely be confiscated.

After you circle around the Old Church, cross the Oudekerksbrug bridge over the canal to the street with the long name of Oudezijds Voorburgwal. Cross the canal. After you've crossed the bridge, head straight to the pedestrian-only Oudekennissteeg. If you turn left onto Oudezijds Achterburgwal, you'll see our next sight at number 54.

The **Erotic Museum** (closed Tuesdays and Wednesdays) shows you the history of S&M, porn, sex shows … you get the picture. Lots of mannequins doing naughty things. It proudly displays erotic drawings by John Lennon.

If you're not interested in visiting the Erotic Museum, turn right from Oudekennissteeg onto Oudezijds Achterburgwal.

Stroll down this street with men looking for some action, others looking to smoke pot, tourists gawking at all of it, and neighborhood residents eating ice cream while pushing baby strollers, oblivious to it all.

As you're walking down the street, you'll pass **Casa Rosso** at 106 Oudezijds Achterburgwal, home to live sex shows. To your left (across from the club) is a fountain in the shape of a penis.

Our final stop is at number 148.

The Hash Marijuana Hemp Museum (Hash Marihuana Hemp Museum) shows you everything you ever wanted to know about cannabis, complete with grow room.

There are plenty of places for you to smoke pot in the area (especially "branches" of Bulldog, said to be the oldest coffeeshop in the city). So if you're inclined to do that, head back to one of the coffeeshops. Or you can head to any number of cafés in the area that can serve you alcoholic or non-alcoholic beverages.

Museum Walk

Highlights: Rijksmuseum, van Gogh Museum, and Film Museum. See Museum Walk map on the next page. Approximate length of walk: one mile.

Take Trams 2 or 5 to the Hobbemastraat/Rijksmuseum stop. This will drop you right in front of the Rijksmuseum. You can also simply walk and follow the signs to the Rijksmuseum.

The impressive Rijksmuseum (Royal Museum) is known for its rich decoration, impressive galleries, and lovely gardens. Even though it's under renovation until 2008, you can visit an exhibit "The Masterpieces" in the already completed Philips Wing of the museum. More than 400 highlights from the Golden Age are on display, including *The Night Watch*, Rembrandt's best-known painting.

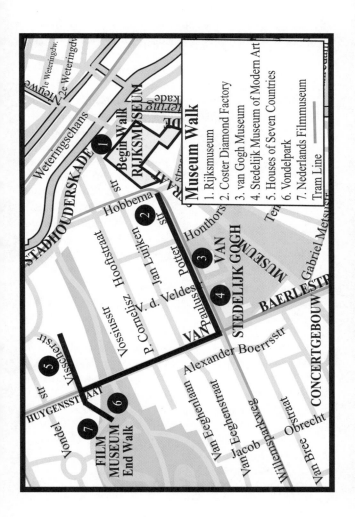

Museum Walk

1. Rijksmuseum
2. Coster Diamond Factory
3. van Gogh Museum
4. Stedelijk Museum of Modern Art
5. Houses of Seven Countries
6. Vondelpark
7. Nederlands Filmmuseum

— Tram Line

Even if you're not interested in visiting the museum, you can visit its gardens.

Behind the museum is an interesting garden that's often overlooked by visitors. Among the fountains and flowers is a display of the ruins of buildings, some dating back to the 17th century, from throughout the Netherlands. Admission to the garden is free.

DETOUR

Stretching from the back of the Rijksmuseum is the city's largest square, the Museumplein. You'll find lots of green grass, a children's playground, and a pond that's an ice-skating rink in the winter.

Head to Paulus Potterstraat.

At number 2 you can tour (for free) the **Coster Diamond Factory**.

Head down the street to the modern building at number 7.

While the Rijksmuseum features the art of many, the van Gogh Museum is mostly devoted to one artist: Vincent van Gogh. More than 200

paintings, nearly 600 drawings and sketches, and hundreds of van Gogh's letters are found here. From his early 1880s paintings to the works of his later years of torment, these works demonstrate not only the development of van Gogh's art, but also of his fascinating life. You may know his famous paintings *Sunflowers* and *Self-Portrait as an Artist*, both of which you will find here, but come to see his other works. In addition to van Gogh's art, the works of such notables as Gauguin, Toulouse-Lautrec, Bernard and Monet are also on display, along with some of van Gogh's extensive collection of Japanese drawings. Don't miss it.

Next door at number 13 Paulus Potterstraat is a contemporary art museum housed in a neo-Renaissance building, the Stedelijk Museum (Municipal Museum). It's currently closed for renovation. Continue down Paulus Potterstraat until you reach Van Baerlestraat. Turn right onto Van Baerlestraat. Pass Jan Luijkenstraat, Peter Cornelisz Hooftstraat, and Vossiusstraat. Turn right onto Roemer Visscherstraat. Head to 20-30 Roemer Visscherstraat.

In less than a block, you can see seven private homes built

in 1894 in the architectural style of seven European countries. At 30 is an English cottage (now a hotel). Also at 30 is a Dutch Renaissance home. At 28 is a Russian cathedral with onion-shaped dome. At 26 is an Italian *palazzo*. At 24 is a pink-and-white striped Spanish villa. At 22 is a French *château*, and at 20 is a German Gothic-style home.

Now head back the way you came on Roemer Visscherstraat, cross Van Baerlestraat and head into the park Vondelpark.

This 120-acre park was named after Joost van den Vondel, known as the "Shakespeare of the Netherlands." In the summer, it's filled with locals enjoying this large green space near the city center.

Take a right and you'll see a 19th-century pavilion. It's home to our final sight.

The Netherlands Film Museum (Nederlands Filmmuseum) is a film museum, library, and a cinema with over 35,000 films. Private screening rooms are available to view videos. The cinema shows everything from silent films from the US to Dutch films. The museum is closed on Sundays and Mondays but the theater is open daily. You can end your walk here at the popular and trendy **Café Vertigo**.

Prinsengracht Canal Walk

Highlights: North Church, West Church, Anne Frank House, and Leidseplein. See Prinsengracht Canal Walk on the next page. Approximate length of walk: two miles.

Our walk begins at the Stationsplein, the bustling square in front of Centraal Station. With Centraal Station to your back, cross the Open Haven Front (that's the body of water right in front of the Stationsplein) until you reach the first street, Prins Hendrikkade. Turn right and continue down Prins Hendrikkade until you reach the Singel, the first canal. Take a left and then a right over the bridge (Haarlemmersluis). On the other side of the bridge, take a left and then a quick right (at the Doors [as in Jim Morrison] Coffeeshop).

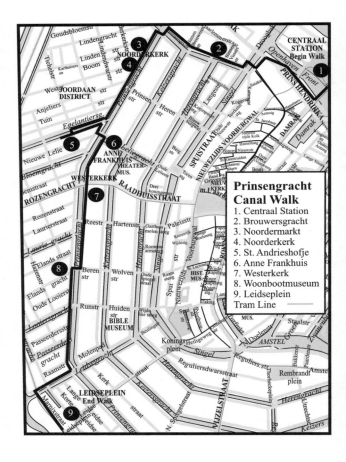

**Prinsengracht
Canal Walk**

1. Centraal Station
2. Brouwersgracht
3. Noordermarkt
4. Noorderkerk
5. St. Andrieshofje
6. Anne Frankhuis
7. Westerkerk
8. Woonbootmuseum
9. Leidseplein

Tram Line ————

The canal that you are now walking along is our first sight.

The tree-lined **Brewers Canal** (Brouwersgracht) is at the northern end of the Jordaan neighborhood. It offers incredibly beautiful views down the four main canals (Prinsengracht, Keizersgracht, Herengracht, and Singel) bordered by impressive buildings. Many think that this canal is the loveliest in the city.

As you walk along the Brouwersgracht, you'll cross the Herengracht (Gentlemen's canal) and the Keizersgracht (Emperor's canal). When you reach the Prinsengracht (Prince's canal), cross the bridge.

If you're in the mood to stop for a coffee or drink, you can check out one of Amsterdam's oldest brown cafés, **Café Papeneiland**, at no. 2. A brown café (*bruine kroeg*) gets its name from the brown tobacco stains on the walls.

After crossing the Prinsengracht canal, turn left, and you'll soon be at our next stop.

The **Northern Market** (Noordermarkt) at Westerstraat is home to a farmers' market on Saturdays. On Monday mornings and early afternoons there's a popular flea market. Looming over the square is the North Church (Noorderkerk), built in the early 17th century in the shape of a Greek cross. It's a premier site for classical concerts. There's a café (**Café Hegeraad**) at the corner of Noordermarkt and Boomstraat that's filled with locals where you might want to stop.

Continue down Prinsengracht.

The first canal to your right is **Egelantiersgracht**. It used to be a drainage ditch. In the 17th century, it was converted into a lovely canal. At number 12, the **Café 't Smalle** is a former distillery and has been open since 1786. There's a nice outdoor terrace along the water where you might want to take a break.

Continue down Egelantiersgracht and take a left over the first bridge (Hilletjesbrug) at Tweede Egelantiersdwarsstraat. Turn right onto Egelantiersgracht and head to number 107.

At 107-114 is **St. Andrieshofje**. Don't be afraid to open the door! Duck into the courtyard of this serene *hofje* (almshouse) dating back to the 1600s and reached through a passageway lined with attractive blue-and-white tiles. Sometimes the door is locked.

After taking in the peaceful courtyard, head back down Egelantiersgracht back to Prinsengracht. Continue down Prinsengracht and cross the canal to the other side at the bridge Leliesluis (that's the bridge where you'll see the restaurant De Prins).

Hungry? Stop in at **Pancake Bakery** at number 191 where you can eat this Dutch favorite with many interesting toppings.

At number 263 is the Anne Frank House (Anne Frankhuis), where the hiding place she so vividly described in her *Diary of Anne Frank* comes to life. Your visit will be poignant and memorable.

Nearby at numbers 279-281 is the West Church (Westerkerk). Hendrick de Keyser, a popular Dutch architect of the Golden Age, designed this Protestant church and the North Church (Noorderkerk) that you saw earlier on this walk. You can't miss its landmark tower, completed in 1631. Step inside and marvel at the ornate organ. Although it's believed that Rembrandt is buried here, only his son's grave is marked.

Further down Prinsengracht,

you'll pass the canal Lauriergracht. Cross over the canal (to your right) at Berenstraat. Opposite 296 Prinsengracht is our next sight.

The **Houseboat Museum** (Woonbootmuseum) lets you experience what life is like on one of the over 2,500 boats that Amsterdammers call home. Open Tuesday to Sunday from March to October, and open Friday to Sunday from November to February.

Continue down Prinsengracht past the canal Passeerdersgracht until you reach the canal Leidsegracht. Turn right on Leidsegracht and walk along the Leidsegracht canal. Turn left at Marnixstraat and walk until you reach the square Leidseplein.

At number 97 Leidsekade is the majestic **American Hotel** where you can pop into the glamorous **Café Americain**, complete with beautiful stained-glass windows and Art Deco interior. You'll feel like you stepped back in time.

You're now at the busy and touristy Leidseplein (Leidse Square). The huge **City Theater** (Stadsschouwburg) at number 26 dominates this square packed with bars and cafés (not to men-tion the nearby **Holland Casino**). Sit down, take in the street performers, and enjoy the end of your walk.

Herengracht Canal Walk

Highlights: Theater Museum, Biblical Museum, Golden Bend, and Rembrandtplein. See Herengracht Canal Walk map on the next page. Approximate length of walk: two miles.

Our walk begins at the Stationsplein, the square in front of Centraal Station. With Centraal Station to your back, cross the Open Haven Front (that's the body of water right in front of the Stationsplein) until you reach the first street, Prins Hendrikkade. Turn right and continue down Prins Hendrikkade.

As you pass the Victoria Hotel, notice the small structures surrounded by the rest of the building. It's said that the owners refused to sell their homes so the builder just decided to build around them

Continue down Prins Hendrikkade until you reach the Singel, the first canal. Take a left and then a right over the

bridge (Haarlemmersluis). On the other side of the bridge, take a left and then a quick right (at the Doors [as in Jim Morrison] Coffeeshop). The canal that you are now walking along is our first sight.

The **Brewers Canal** (Brouwersgracht), lined with trees, is at the northern end of the Jordaan neighborhood. It offers incredibly beautiful views down the canal.

At Herengracht, you'll be at the square Herenmarkt. Turn right and pass the children's playground. This building is the **Westindisch Huis**, the former headquarters of the Dutch West Indies Company. If you want to step back in time, you can pop into its courtyard (at number 99). The sale of Manhattan occurred here, and the decision to transfer West Africans to the Caribbean as slaves was also made here. In the courtyard is a fountain and statue of Peter Stuyvesant, who became di-

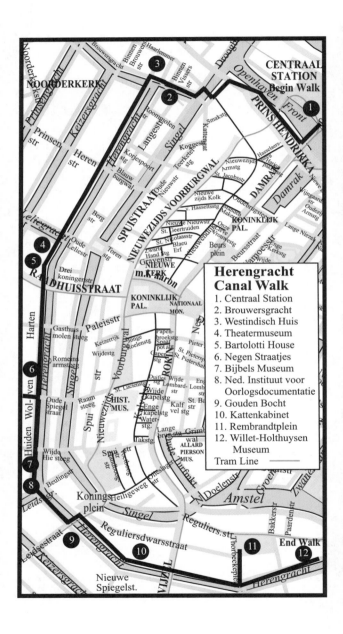

CENTRAAL STATION
Begin Walk

Herengracht Canal Walk

1. Centraal Station
2. Brouwersgracht
3. Westindisch Huis
4. Theatermuseum
5. Bartolotti House
6. Negen Straatjes
7. Bijbels Museum
8. Ned. Instituut voor Oorlogsdocumentatie
9. Gouden Bocht
10. Kattenkabinet
11. Rembrandtplein
12. Willet-Holthuysen Museum

Tram Line ———

rector of all Dutch possessions in North America (and governor of New York).

Retrace your steps to Brouwersgracht. You'll cross the canal and turn left onto Herengracht. Walk down the Herengracht. You'll walk a while before you reach our next sight.

Get ready to see some spectacular architecture. At number 168 (just after Leliegracht) is the Theater Museum (Theatermuseum), closed weekend mornings. These beautiful canal houses are home to a museum showcasing the performance arts, with everything from puppets to opera costumes to set designs. But if you ask me, the building and its period garden are the real stars.

Next door at 170-172, you can't miss the Dutch Renaissance façade and red brick gable of the **Bartolotti House**. You can walk through its richly decorated interior if you're visiting the Theatermuseum.

At number 262, look left across the canal at the house on the corner.

No, you didn't have too much to drink. The house is tipsy, not you. Homes here were built on wood pilings that went down through soft soil to a firm layer of sand. Over the years, some of the pilings (and houses) have shifted.

DETOUR

At Wolvenstraat, turn right and visit one of the interesting shops here. This is one of the Negen Straatjes (Nine Streets) that are loaded with specialty shops, and are a nice break from the department and chain stores found in other shopping areas of the city. Check out the beautiful hand-embroidered white tablecloths found at Laura Dols, *Tel. 020/624-9066*, 6-7 Wolvenstraat, and the tassel shop (I'm not kidding), H.J. van de Kerkhof, *Tel. 020/623-4666*, 9-11 Wolvenstraat.

Our next stop is farther down Herengracht at number 366-368 at Huidenstraat.

The Biblical Museum (Bijbels Museum), appropriately closed on Sunday mornings) is housed in two 17th-century buildings. The museum is packed with archeological finds, religious objects, centuries-old models of histori-cal religious sites, and arti-facts from ancient Egypt and the Middle East.

Further down Herengracht at number 380, history buffs re-search the archives of the **Netherlands Institute for War Documentation** (Nederlands Instituut voor Oorlogsdocumentatie). Take in the fantastic castle-like exterior with sculptures of mythical figures.

Continue down Herengracht where the canal begins to bend at Leidsegracht. Turn left on the next bridge (at Leidsestraat) and cross the canal. Turn right onto Herengracht.

The bend in the canal is called the Golden Bend (Gouden Bocht). It was here where the bigwigs built their homes in the 17th and 18th centuries. They remain today for you take in all their beauty, espe-cially number 475 in the over-the-top Louis XVI style.

If you're a cat lover, you can stop at number 497.

The **Cat Cabinet** (Kattenkabinet) is the only museum in the world to feature a collection of paint-ings and other art objects de-voted solely to cats, from Egyp-tian bronze statues to *Le Chat* by Picasso (closed Saturday and Sun-day mornings).

As you continue down Herengracht, you'll pass Vijzelstraat. The next canal you cross is Reguliersgracht.

Stop on the bridge here with your back to the square Thorbeckeplein and look down the Reguliersgracht ca-nal. From here, you can see quite a few of Amsterdam's 1,281 bridges!

Now head into Thorbeckeplein (the square that was to your back as you looked at the bridges) and then into Rembrandtplein.

A statue of Rembrandt was placed in this square, Rembrandtplein, in 1876. It used to be called "Botermarkt" after the butter market that was held here. Today, it's a lively place filled with out-door cafés. One of them, with its balcony overlooking the square, is **De Kroon** at num-ber 17. You'll know it when you see its waiters in long white aprons serving custom-ers beneath crystal chande-liers. Why don't you take a break here?

This can be the end of your

walk or you can head back to Herengracht and continue down to number 605 near the Amstel River.

The **Willet-Holthuysen Museum** is a restored canal house dating back to 1687. There are a series of period rooms loaded with tapestries, Delft china, portraits, and a lot of stuff that must take a long time to dust.

You can end your walk at the Amstel River, just down the Herengracht.

Keizersgracht Canal Walk

Highlights: House With the Heads, the Van Loon Museum, and the Skinny Bridge. See Keizersgracht Canal Walk on the next page. Approximate length of walk: two and a half miles.

Our walk begins at the Stationsplein, the bustling square in front of Centraal Station. With Centraal Station to your back, cross the Open Haven Front (that's the body of water right in front of the Stationsplein) until you reach the first street, Prins Hendrikkade. Turn right and continue down Prins Hendrikkade until you reach the Singel, the first canal. Take a left and then a right over the bridge (Haarlemmersluis). On the other side of the bridge, take a left and then a quick right (at the Doors [as in Jim Morrison] Coffeeshop).

The canal that you are now walking along is our first sight.

The **Brewers Canal** (Brouwersgracht), lined with trees, is at the northern end of the Jordaan neighborhood.

You'll cross the Herengracht (Gentlemen's canal) and then cross Keizersgracht. Turn left. Continue to number 82.

The **Galerie Binnen** displays changing exhibits of modern international designers.

Continue down Keizersgracht. After you cross Prinsenstraat, look to your left over the canal at number 123. It's the house with the heads on it.

The House With the Heads (Huis met de Hoofden) is a

Keizersgracht Canal Walk

1. Centraal Station
2. Brouwersgracht
3. Huis met de Hoofden
4. Amsterdam School of Architecture Building
5. Westerkerk
6. Homomonument
7. Felix Meritis Building
8. Negen Straatjes
9. Huis Marseille
10. Metz & Co.
11. Museum Van Loon
12. Magere Brug
Tram Line ———

grand mansion built in the 1620s. It obviously gets its name from the six heads featured on its elaborate exterior. They are said to represent the deities Apollo, Ceres, Mars, Minerva, Diana and Bacchus, but legend has it that they really represent burglars who had their heads chopped off by a maid! The building is not open to the public.

Further down Keizersgracht is our next sight at 174-176, at the corner of Leliegracht.

This building is an excellent example of the Amsterdam school of architecture. Its most recent tenant was the non-profit environmental group Greenpeace.

Continue down Keizersgracht until you reach the square Westermarkt.

At the corner of Keizersgracht and Raadhuisstraat and next to the **West Church** (Westerkerk) is a monument of three pink granite triangles, representing the pink triangles homosexuals were forced to wear during the Nazi occupation. The **Homosexual Monument** (Homomonument) remembers homosexuals who were rounded up and sent to concentration camps. There's an information booth here for gay visitors to the city.

Next, take a look at number 268.

See that gold chain hanging from the front? Legend has it that the owner of the canal house couldn't find her gold chain and blamed the maid of stealing it. When the owner found it, the chain was hung on the gable as proof of the maid's innocence. Another version of the legend also involves the maid. She is said to have killed a burglar, and the owner gave her a gold chain in thanks. When she refused it (thinking it wasn't enough of a reward), the owner hung it to show his irritation with the maid. It's most likely that it was simply hung as decoration.

Next, take a look at number 324.

The **Felix Meritis Building** (open for events only) is an impressive neo-Classical building built in 1787, and was the home of a society of wealthy residents of Amsterdam called the Felix Meritis Society. The name means "happiness through merit." The society survives today, and is dedicated to connecting the world's cultures. Its opulent Shaffy Theater with excellent acoustics still hosts performances.

At number 384 is the courtyard of the popular Dylan Hotel (formerly Blakes), also home to an elegant restaurant.

DETOUR

If you take a right at Runstraat you'll be on one of the Negen Straatjes (Nine Streets) loaded with specialty shops and restaurants. At number 5 is De Witte Tanden Winkel, a shop with a huge selection of toothbrushes and toothpaste of every imaginable flavor. At number 13 is Lust, an inexpensive place for lunch with pasta dishes, salads, and stir-fry dishes.

Turn left at Runstraat and cross the canal to the other side. Turn right onto Keizersgracht.

At numbers 369-371, you'll see another excellent example of the Amsterdam school of architecture. Notice the striking stained-glass window that runs several stories on this 1938 building.

Continue down Keizersgracht until you reach number 401.

Street numbers weren't used until 1795. Before this, buildings were identified by wall plaques. They frequently identified not only the house, but featured the religion, occupation, or origin of the owner. The wall plaque at **Huis Marseille** is just such an example. The stone tablet on the façade (above and to the left of the door) has a plan of the city of Marseille, France, and dates back to 1665 when the canal house was built by a wealthy French merchant. The building is now occupied by the Foundation for Photography, which changes its interesting photography exhibits every three months.

Our next stop is at number 455 on the corner of Leidsegracht.

Metz & Co is Amsterdam's upscale department store. Lots of luxury household goods and designer clothes. Take the stairs or elevator to the 6th floor where between 9:30am and 5:45pm you'll get a free view of the city and can have a drink at the penthouse café. You'll really enjoy the view.

Continue down the Keizersgracht and cross the canal to your right at Vijzelstraat. Turn left onto Keizersgracht. At number 672 is a favorite museum of many visitors to Amsterdam.

The **Van Loon Museum**, an old canal house built in 1672, closed Tuesday, Wednesday and Thursday, lets you step back in time to the Dutch Golden Age. It was inhabited by the van Loon family from 1884 to 1945. The mansion contains furnishings and art, and has a lovely rose garden. There are also portraits of the families who called this their home over the ages.

Head down to the corner of Keizersgracht and Utrechtsestraat (at 61 Utrechtsestraat).

What's that delicious smell? Stop in for some great pastry at **Willem Van Eÿk**, a wonderful Dutch bakery.

Continue down Keizersgracht until you reach the Amstel River. Make a right and you'll be facing our next sight.

The not really so skinny **Skinny Bridge** (Magere Brug) is said to have been built in the 17th century by the Magere sisters who lived across the Amstel River from each other and were too lazy to walk far to visit. Others believe the bridge got its name from the word mager (which means skinny or narrow). Either way, it's a great photo opportunity. Built in the traditional Dutch drawbridge style, it's raised frequently to allow boats to pass. The bridge that's in place today was constructed in 1969. What a typical Dutch scene, and what a great way to end our walk.

3. MISCELLANY

Dining

Beyond the simple pleasure of eating, dining in a foreign country gives you an insight into the soul of its people. It's a glimpse of their customs, their likes and dislikes, their foibles, their accomplishments. It puts you in contact with local culture.

Go ahead and admit that you have a bad impression of Dutch food. You probably think of lots of over-cooked vegetables, starchy dishes and raw herring. Although Dutch cuisine isn't the favorite of most, the Dutch have embraced world cuisine, especially Indonesian food, and you'll find a wide variety of all types of dishes in Amsterdam. Dutch explorers brought back exotic spices (such as curry, nutmeg, and ginger), and you'll find them used liberally in modern Dutch cuisine.

Get ready for a large breakfast (meat, cheese and bread), light lunches, and early dining. The Dutch eat dinner as early as 5:30 p.m. If you're not into early dining, many cafés have long service hours.

There's no need to spend a lot of money in Amsterdam to have good food. There are all kinds of fabulous foods to be had inexpensively.

Eat at a neighborhood restaurant. You'll always know the price of a meal before entering, as almost all restaurants

RESTAURANT PRICES

Restaurant prices in this book are for a main course and without wine:

Inexpensive:
under €10
Moderate: €11-€20
Expensive: €21-€30
Very Expensive:
over €30

post the menu and prices in the window. Never order anything whose price is not known in advance.

Delis and food stores can provide cheap and wonderful meals. Buy some cheese, bread, wine and other snacks and have a picnic in one of Amsterdam's great parks. Remember to pack a corkscrew and eating utensils when you leave home. Lunch, even at the most expensive restaurants listed in this guide, always has a lower fixed price.

Restaurants near tourist attractions are almost always more expensive than neighborhood restaurants and bistros.

Street vendors in Amsterdam generally sell inexpensive and good food. You should definitely try *broodjes*, small cheese and/or cold-cut sandwiches. The Dutch eat their french fries (sold by many street vendors) with mayonnaise.

For the cost of a cup of coffee or a drink, you can linger at a café and watch the world pass you by for as long as you want. It's one of Amsterdam's greatest bargains.

Know what you're ordering. Here are a few food and drink specialties of Amsterdam:
- **advocaat**, egg liqueur
- **appelgebak**, apple pastry
- **bier**, the Dutch are known for their beer. Can you say "Heineken"?
- **bitterballen**, deep-fried meatballs or potato balls
- **capucijners met spek**, beans with bacon
- **chocola**, don't leave Amsterdam without tasting some great Dutch chocolate!
- **drop**, salty licorice
- **erwtensoep**, thick and creamy pea soup with chunks of ham, potatoes, and carrots
- **gember met slagroom**, slices of fresh ginger, topped with whipped cream.

THE BORREL

The Dutch have a tradition of having a drink (*borrel*) at around 5:00pm. It can be a glass of wine, a mug of beer or a bit of gin (*jenever*), with nuts, cheese and/or crackers, sort of like Spanish *tapas*. Often, the drink is accompanied by deep-fried meatballs (*bitterballen*) that are dipped in mustard. So after a day of scurrying around town, take a break and enjoy a *borrel*!

•**gerookte paling**, smoked eel
•**hazepeper**, bunny!
•**hutspot**, beef, potato, onion, and carrot stew
•**jenever**, gin
•**kaas**, cheese. The Dutch have great cheese, as good as Wisconsin (where I'm from)
•**krabbetjes**, spareribs
•**krokette**, deep-fried dumpling
•**maatjesharing**, raw herring
•**mosselen**, mussels
•**muisjes**, candied anise seeds
•**osseworst**, spiced smoked beef sausage
•**pannenkoeken**, pancakes
•**patat**, french fries (usually served with mayonnaise)
•**poffertjes**, small pieces of fried pancake mixture topped with sugar
•**rijsttafel**, Indonesian specialty of fish, meat and veg-etables with sauces and rice. The Dutch have been lovers of Indonesian foods since colonial times, and Indonesia was a colony until 1949
•**rolpens**, minced beef, red cabbage, and fried apples
•**saucijzenbroodje**, sausage roll
•**speculaas/spekulaas**, spicy biscuits
•**stampot**, cabbage with smoked sausage
•**stroopwafels**, waffle cookies
•**tosties**, grilled sandwiches (usually ham and cheese)
•**uitsmijter**, a slice of bread topped with ham, roast beef and/or cheese and topped with a fried egg
•**zuurkool met worst en speck**, sauerkraut with sausage and bacon

Amsterdam by Season

Winter

Parcel Evening (Pakjesavond) on December 5. We give presents on Christmas Day, but the Dutch give them much earlier.

New Year's Eve (Oudejaarsavond) on December 31. It's wild here on New Year's Eve (and into New Year's Day). Everyone, and I mean everyone, is in the streets. There are fireworks everywhere, some being set off right next to you.

Spring

Tulips, tulips and more tulips! Amsterdammers break out of their winter doldrums.

Silent Procession (Stille Omgang) on the Sunday closest to March 15. This procession begins near the Royal Palace at midnight. Catholics walk in silence along the Holy Way (Heiligeweg) in celebration of the 1345 "Miracle of the Host" when a dying man puked a communion host into a fire, but it emerged undamaged (and the man survived).

National Museum Weekend *(www.museumweekend.nl)* one weekend in April. Museums allow free (or deeply discounted) admission and extended hours.

Queen's Day (Koninginnedag) on April 30. A wild celebration (everyone is in the streets) of the Queen's birthday (actually the birthday of the Queen's mother, Queen Juliana). Don't forget to wear orange, because the royal family is from the House of Orange.

World Press Photo Exhibition from mid-April to mid-May. The Old Church (Oude Kerk) displays the cream of the crop of newspaper and magazine photography from the past year.

Open Garden Days in May. Private canal-house gardens throughout the city are open to the public.

Remembrance Day (Herdenkingsdag) and **Liberation Day** (Bevrijdingsdag) on May 4 and 5. Amsterdam celebrates the liberation from Nazi occupation. The Queen lays a wreath at the National Monument, and the country observes a poignant two-minute silence on Remembrance Day at 8 p.m. Huge street celebrations erupt on Liberation Day. For you Canadians, you'll see your flag being waived by Amsterdammers. That's because the Canadians were the first troops to arrive here.

National Cycling Day on the second Saturday in May. Only in the Netherlands would there be a day to celebrate bicycles! Hope you aren't driving a car on this day.

Canal Run (Amsterdamse Grachtenloop) in late May/early June. A 5km or 10km run along the city's canals begins at Stadsschouwburg on the Leidseplein. The race route is a total party zone.

Summer

The **Holland Festival** held the entire month of June. An arts festival with an emphasis on dance, opera, and theater at venues throughout the city.

The **World Roots Festival** for nine days in early- to mid-June *(www.melkweg.nl)*. A celebration of film, dance, music, and theater from all over the world, and especially non-Western cultures. Centered around De Melkweg (a multimedia center in the southern Canal Belt).

Summer Arts Festival during July. Dance, music, and theater, with an emphasis on the avant-garde, at venues all around town.

Parade (De Parade) through the month of August. An outdoor theater festival featuring everything from performance art to cabaret, held along the Amstel River on the southern part of town at the Martin Luther Kingpark. There's a huge beer tent, too.

Gay Pride Parade the first Saturday in August. Tolerant Amsterdam is a huge destination for gay travelers, and especially so during the Gay Pride celebration. In Amsterdam's version, the parade is on boats along the Prinsengracht.

Entertainment Market (Uitmarkt) during the last week of August. Outdoor stages (especially in Dam Square, Museumplein and Leidseplein) are set up throughout the city to preview the coming cultural season, from pop to opera.

Autumn

Flower Parade (Bloemen Corso) on the first Saturday of September. A parade of floats filled with fragrant flowers travels from Aalsmeer, the flower capital of the Netherlands, to Dam Square.

Open Monument Day (Open Monumentendag) is usually the second weekend in September. You can visit national monuments and historic buildings not usually open to the public.

The **Jordaan Street Festival** is usually the third weekend in September. A lively neighborhood street festival centered along Elandsgracht in the Jordaan neighborhood

Amsterdam Marathon in mid-October. Runners descend on Amsterdam for one of the world's fastest (and flattest) courses.

Museum Night in November. Museums open their doors to the public at night.

Santa Claus (Sinterklaas) arrives in mid-November. The beginning of the holiday season starts with the arrival of St. Nicholas on a steamboat at Centraal Station. Then he rides through the city on a white horse with Black Pete, whoever the hell that is. Actually, Black Pete is his helper who is black from climbing up and down all those chimneys. Sinterklaas is given the keys to the city on Dam Square.

Airports & Getting Around

Airports/Arrivals

Schiphol Airport, only 8 miles (13 km) from central Amsterdam, is one of the busiest in the world. It's also one of the most convenient. To reach Centraal Station (the main train station in Amsterdam), trains depart from the airport train station (downstairs from Schiphol Plaza) every 15 minutes (hourly 1am-5am). Get on the train that says "Amsterdam CS." The one-way fare is less than €4. It's very easy and convenient to use, and the trains are clearly marked. There are kiosks that allow you to buy train tickets (with instructions in English). A taxi costs nearly €40 to central Amsterdam. Buses are slower, and depart from Schiphol Plaza. They aren't much cheaper than the train. There's a hotel shuttle bus (Connexxion) that operates from Schiphol Plaza that takes you to about 20 main hotels for around €9 (buy the ticket on the bus).

Cars & Driving

Are you crazy? Parking is chaotic, gas is extremely expensive, and driving in Amsterdam is an unpleasant "adventure." With the incredible public transportation system, there's absolutely no reason to rent a car. If you drive to your hotel, park it and leave it there, and use public transportation or your feet. By the way, one kilometer equals .62 miles. To convert miles to kilometers, multiply by 1.61. So, one mile equals 1.61 kilometers.

Canal Tours

Amsterdam can be a confusing city. With its maze of canals and streets, a good way to get your bearings is to take one of the many canal tours that dock near Centraal Station and along Damrak, the main street. These glass-topped boats designed to easily get under the bridges are called *rondvaarten*. Yes, it may be touristy, but it's a great way to see the city. The typical trip lasts about an hour and comes with recorded commentary in English (and tons of other languages). You really get a wonderful view of the bridges and houses that line the canals. Some boats also offer meals and drinks. Tours begin at €7.

Bike Rentals

You may look on in horror at the thousands of bicyclists crisscrossing with speeding automobiles in Amsterdam. Locals use their bikes as a main source of transportation and are experts at managing the traffic. There are special bike lanes everywhere with their own bicycle traffic signals. If you think you're up to it, try renting a bike. It can be great fun and an easy way to see a lot of the city. One company, **Mac Bike** *(www.macbike.nl)*, rents for a minimum of two hours, by the day, and longer. Daily rental prices begin at €7

for a standard bicycle with footbrake. There are three locations:

•*Central Station Eastpoint (next to Centraal Station): 12 Stationsplein, Tel. 020/624-8391;*

•*2 Mr. Visserplein (metro to Waterlooplein), Tel. 020/620-0985; and*

•*2 Weteringschans (tram stop Leidseplein), Tel. 020/528-7688.*

They will hold your passport and €50 or an imprint of your credit card as a deposit. As bike theft is a problem, make sure you get insurance. This particular company charges the daily rate plus 50% to insure the bike. I rented two bikes for a day with insurance

---

THOSE CONFUSING STREET NAMES!

The end of every street name tells you a lot about the street:

gracht means canal
kade means a street that runs parallel to a canal
laan means avenue
markt means market
plein means square
steeg is an alley or lane
straat means street
straatje is a small street

for €18. See Amsterdam as the locals do!

Public Transportation

Don't be afraid to use public transportation. It's not that hard to figure out. Trams are frequent and easy-to-use. They run until shortly after midnight. Buses fill the gap between 1 and 6am. On Sundays, trams don't run until 7:30am. Amsterdam's partly underground Metro (subway) is used mostly for travel to the suburbs. You can buy a tram ticket from the driver or, on some trams, from a machine in the middle of it. You can buy a *strippenkaart* from the post office, rail and bus stations, or tobacco shops. These cards are based on zones. If you stay in central Amsterdam, you'll be in zone one. Each trip is one strip. You stamp the ticket in the yellow machine on the tram. More than one person can use the card. You just stamp it for how ever many people are using it. Once stamped, the ticket is valid for one hour (including all transfers). A single ticket cost €1.60. An eight-strip card costs €5.60, a 15-strip card costs €6.40, and a 45–strip card costs €17.40. There are also day and week passes available. Stops are announced and posted as you approach.

Museumboot
(Museum Boat)
Prins Hendrikkade in front of Centraal Station
Tel. 020/530-1090
Open daily 10am-5pm
Admission: €14, €9 ages 4-12, under 12 free (includes a discount on museum admission). After 1pm, you can purchase cheaper "stop tickets," based on how many stops you intend to make.

Take a canal boat to many of Amsterdam's most popular museums. There are seven stops:

1: Centraal Station: Departure point
2: Westermarkt: Anne Frank House, Theatermuseum
3: Leidseplein: Vondelpark
4: Museum Quarter: van Gogh Museum, Rijksmuseum, Stedelijk Museum
5: Herengracht: Flower Market, Amsterdams Historisch Museum, Bijbels Museum
6: Waterlooplein: Jewish Historical Museum, Museum Het Rembrandthuis, Muziektheater, Tropenmuseum, Artis
7: Eastern Docks: NEMO, Maritime Museum

Canal Bikes
(Pedal Boats)
Rental shops located near the Anne Frank House, Rijksmuseum,

Leidseplein, and the corner of Keizersgracht and Leidsestraat
Tel. 020/626-5574
Open daily Apr-Oct 10am-6pm (July and Aug until 9:30pm)
Admission: €8 per hour, €7 per hour for three or more. €50 deposit required
www.canal.nl

If you thought the canal boat tours made you look like a tourist, wait till you see the pedal boats called "canal bikes" or *waterfiets*! Most have four seats and rain shields.

Canal Bus

3 route lines throughout town with stops at most major sights
Tel. 020/626-5574 or 623-9886
Admission: €16 day pass, €11 ages 4-13, under 4 free (coupon book included)
www.canal.nl

Pretend you're in Venice and take the water bus! You can buy a day pass and get off and on as often as you like. There are 14 stops. An interesting way to get around town.

Ferries

Departing from the piers behind Centraal Station

Take in great views of the port and shipyards on a ferry for free. The IJ channel lies between Central Amsterdam and Amsterdam Nord (North Amsterdam), and crossing it takes a little over five minutes. The **Buiksloterwegveer** ferry departs daily from Pier 7 every 15 minutes during the day and every half-hour in the evening. A smaller ferry, the **IJ-Veer**, departs from Pier 8 every 15 minutes weekdays from 6am to 6pm. The **Java Ferry** departs from Pier 8 to the new island of Java which is filled with interesting modern architecture (departure times vary). All ferries allow bicycles on them.

Other Basic Information

Customs

Citizens of the US who have been away more than 48 hours can bring home $800 of merchandise duty-free every 30 days. For more information, go to Traveler Information ("Know Before You Go") at www.customs.gov. Canadians can bring back C\$750 each year if you've been gone for 7 days or more.

Electricity

The electrical current in Amsterdam is 220 volts as opposed to 110 volts found in North America. Don't fry your electric razor, hairdryer or laptop. You'll need a converter and an adapter. Some laptops don't require a converter, but why are you bringing that anyway?

Embassies/Consulates

US Consulate in Amsterdam: *19 Museumplein, Tel. 020/ 575-5309*

Canadian Embassy in The Hague: *7 Sophialaan, Tel. 070/311-1600*

E-Mail

Cyber cafés seem to pop up everywhere (and go out of business quickly). You shouldn't have difficulty finding a place to e-mail home. The going rate is about €2 per hour.

Holidays

January 1: New Year's Day
Good Friday: (movable day)
Easter and the Monday after Easter: (movable day)
Ascension Day (40 days after Easter): (movable day)

April 30: Queen's Day
May 4: Remembrance Day
May 5: Liberation Day
Pentecost Monday: (movable day)
December 25: Christmas
December 26

Note that many restaurants are closed between Christmas and New Year's Eve.

Insurance

Check with your health care provider. Most policies don't cover you overseas. If that's the case, you may want to obtain medical insurance (one such provider is found at www.medexassist.com). Given the uncertainties in today's world, you may also want to purchase trip-cancellation insurance (one provider is www.travelguard.com). Make sure that your policy covers sickness, disasters, bankruptcy and State Department travel restrictions and warnings. In other words, read the fine print!

Language/Useful Phrases

Although nearly everyone speaks English, this book has a list of helpful Dutch phrases. It's always courteous to learn a few. Below are some helpful Dutch phrases:

Note: the sound of e as in

monster (with a silent r) is represented by a red e.

please, *alstublieft* (ahls-te-bleeft)
thank you, *dank u wel* (dahnk-ou-wel)
yes, *ja* (yah)
no, *nee* (nay)
hello, *hallo or dag* (hullo or dahg)
good morning, *goedemorgen* (goode-mor-ghen)
good evening, *goedenavond* (goodenahvont)
goodbye, *tot ziens* (tot zeens)

what, *wat* (wot)
where is, *waar is* (wahr is)
Do you speak English?, *Spreekt U Engels?* (spraykt ou eng-els)
I don't understand, *Ik begrijp het niet* (ik beghrehp et neet)
excuse me, *Pardon* (pahr-don)
Help, *Help* (help)
I am sick, *Ik ben ziek* (ik ben zeek)
Where are the restrooms, *Waar is de WC* (wahr is de way-say)

I'd like a table, *Is er een tafel vrij?* (is er en tahfel vraiy)
I'd like to reserve a table, *Ik wil een tafel reserveren* (ik wil en tahfel ray- ser-vehren)
Check/bill, *de rekening* (de rehkening)

Numbers:
1: een (ayn)
2: twee (tway)
3: drie (dree)
4: vier (veer)
5: vijf (vehf)
6: zes (zess)
7: zeven (zayven)
8: acht (ahgt)
9: negen (nay-gen)
10: tien (teen)

open, *geopend* (ghe-oh-pent)
closed, *gesloten* (ghe-slohten)
How much does this cost?, *Hoeveel kost dit?* (hoo-vehl kost dit)

Monday, *maandag* (mahn-dagh)
Tuesday, *dinsdag* (dins-dagh)
Wednesday, *woensdag* (woons-dagh)
Thursday, *donderdag* (donder-dagh)
Friday, *vrijdag* (vreh-dagh)
Saturday, *zaterdag* (zahter-dagh)
Sunday, *zondag* (zon-dagh)

Money

The **euro** (**€**) is the currency of the Netherlands and most of Europe. Before you leave for Amsterdam, it's a good idea to get some euros. It makes your arrival a lot easier. Call your credit-card company or bank before you leave to tell them that you'll be using your ATM or credit card outside the country. Many have automatic controls that can "freeze" your account if the computer program determines that there are charges outside your normal area. ATMs (of course, with fees) are the easiest way to change money in Amsterdam. You'll find them everywhere. The Dutch call ATMs *"pin automaat"* or *"pin"* for short. You can still get traveler's checks, but why bother?

Museums

The **"I Amsterdam Card"** (formerly Amsterdam Pass) is an incredible deal. It's available from tourist information offices and online at *www.amsterdam.info/pass*. It includes public transportation (with the exception of transportation between the city and the airport), admission to most museums and attractions, and a coupon book (including a free canal tour). Three different types are available: 24 hours (€33), 48 hours (€43) or 72 hours (€53).

Packing

Never pack prescription drugs, eyeglasses or valuables. Carry them on. Think black. It always works for men and women. Oh, and by the way, pack light. Don't ruin your trip by having to lug around huge suitcases. Before you leave home, make copies of your passport, airline tickets and confirmation of hotel reservations. You should also make a list of your credit-card numbers and the telephone numbers for your credit-card companies. If you lose any of them (or they're stolen), you can call someone at home and have them provide the information to you. You should also pack copies of these documents separate from the originals.

Passports

You'll need a valid passport to enter the Netherlands from the US and Canada for visits under three months. No visa is required.

Restrooms

There aren't a lot of public restrooms (*toiletten*). If you need to go, your best bet is to head (no pun intended) to the nearest café. It's considered good manners to purchase something if you use the restroom. If there's an attendant, tip up to €0.50. By the way, if you choose to pee in public, the fine is at least €40. For men, there are quite a few metal or plastic outdoor urinals, especially in areas where there are lots of tourist attractions.

Running

Amsterdam is a hard city to run in (except perhaps early

Sunday morning). Two parks where you can run are Vondelpark and Amsterdamse Bos.

Safety

Don't wear a "fanny pack;" it's a sign that you're a tourist and an easy target (especially in crowded tourist areas). Avoid wearing expensive jewelry. If you go to the Red-Light District in the evening, be careful and watch your wallet.

Shopping

Throughout this guide, you'll find recommended places to shop. Most shops in Amsterdam are closed on Monday mornings. The Dutch shop at **HEMA Department Stores** and you should check them out, too. They're all over town.

Taxes

Hotel and restaurant prices are required by law to include taxes and service charges. **Value Added Tax (BTW)** is nearly 20% (higher on luxury goods). The BTW is included in the price of goods. Foreigners are entitled to a refund, but must fill out a refund form. When you make your purchase, you should ask for the form and instructions if you're purchasing €137 or more in one place

and in one day (no combining). Yes, it can be a hassle. Check *www.globalrefund.com* for the latest information on refunds (and help for a fee).

Telephone

•Country code for the Netherlands: 31
•Area code for Amsterdam: 020
•Calling Amsterdam from the US and Canada: dial 011-31-20 plus the seven-digit local number
•Calling the US or Canada from Amsterdam: dial 00 (wait for the tone), dial 1 plus the area code and seven-digit local number
•Calling Amsterdam from other towns in the Netherlands: dial 020 plus the seven-digit local number
•Calling within Amsterdam: dial the seven-digit local number.

Phone cards purchased in Amsterdam are the cheapest way to call. US-issued calling cards can be terribly expensive to use from Amsterdam.

Time

When it's noon in New York City, it's 6pm in Amsterdam. For hours of events or schedules, the Dutch use the 24-hour clock. So 6am is 06h00 and 1pm is 13h00.

Tipping

All prices at hotels and restaurants in Amsterdam include tax and tip. It's the law. In restaurants, it's common to tip up to a maximum of 10%. In bars and cafés, it's common to round up and leave the change. It's common to tip taxi drivers up to 10%. If you see the abbreviation BTW, that means that tax and tip are included. The attendant in a restroom expects up to €0.50. If a doorman calls a cab for you, tip €1 to €1.50. Tip coat check €0.50 to €1. Bellhops expect €1 per bag.

Water

Tap water is safe in Amsterdam.

Web Sites

City of Amsterdam: *w w w . a m s t e r d a m . n l*; *www.visitamsterdam.nl* US State Department Foreign Entry Requirements: *h t t p : / / t r a v e l . s t a t e . g o v / foreignentryreqs.html*

Weather

Temperatures dip to around freezing in winter. Fall and spring are pleasant, but can be wet. Summer is very pleasant. Average high temperature/low temperature/days of rain:

January: 41º (5ºC)/34º (1ºC)/ 22

February: 42º (5ºC)/32º (0ºC)/19

March: 48º (8ºC)/37º (2ºC)/ 15

April: 53º (11ºC)/40º (4ºC)/ 16

May: 61º (16ºC)/46º (7ºC)/ 14

June: 66º (18ºC)/52º (11ºC)/ 14

July: 69º (20ºC)/55º (12ºC)/ 17

August: 70º (21ºC)/55º (12ºC)/18

September: 64º (17ºC)/51º (10ºC)/19

October: 57º (13ºC)/46º (7ºC)/20

November: 48º (8ºC)/39º (3ºC)/21

December: 44º (6ºC)/36º (2ºC)/21

Accommodations

Prices are for two people in a double room.

Expensive (over €200)
717
717 Prinsengracht

Tel. 020/427-0717
www.717hotel.nl

Barbizon Palace
58-72 Prins Hendrikkade
Tel. 020/556-4564
www.nh-hotels.com

Dylan (formerly Blakes)
384 Keizersgracht
Tel. 020/530-2010
www.dylanamsterdam.com

Pulitzer
315-331 Prinsengracht
Tel. 020523-5235
www.luxurycollection.com/
pulitzer

Moderate (€125-200)
Eden
144 Amstel
Tel. 020/530-7878
www.bestwestern.nl

Piet Hein
52-53 Vossiusstraat
Tel. 020/662-7205
www.hotelpiethein.com

Prinsen
36-38 Vondelstraat
Tel. 020/616-2323
www.prinsenhotel.nl

Wiechmann
328-32 Prinsengracht
Tel. 020/626-3321
www.hotelwiechmann.nl

Inexpensive (under €125)
Agora
462 Singel
Tel. 020/627-2200
www.hotelagora.nl

Rembrandt
17 Plantage Middenlaan
Tel. 020/627-2714
www.hotelrembrandt.nl

Truelove Guesthouse
4 Prinsenstraat
Tel. 020/320-2500
www.truelove.be

Washington
10 Frans van Mierisstraat
Tel. 020/679-7453
www.hotelwashington.nl

INDEX

Made Easy Guides

The World's Best Sights & Walks–Made Easy!

Amsterdam
Berlin
London
New York City
Paris
Rome
Provence & the French Riviea

New from Open Road Publishing

Available wherever books are sold, and at
www.eatndrink.com, www.amazon.com, www.bn.com,
and www.simonsays.com